MEMORY
PUZZLES

SIRIUS

SIRIUS

This edition published in 2019 by Sirius Publishing, a division of
Arcturus Publishing Limited,
26/27 Bickels Yard, 151–153 Bermondsey Street,
London SE1 3HA

ISBN: 978-1-78950-711-9
AD006845NT

Printed in China

Contents

Instructions

How good is your memory?

Do you find yourself forgetting why you went into a room, or wondering what it was you intended to buy at the supermarket? If so, then welcome to the club – you're just like most of the rest of us!

We all forget things from time to time, but the good news is that it doesn't have to be that way. It turns out that, with just a little practice, we can all learn to make much better use of our memories.

In this book, we'll take a look at various techniques you can use, as well as learn a little about your memory too. We'll also include a large number of exercises so you can try out your memorization and recall skills on a wide range of subjects, and in a great variety of different ways. Usually these exercises will be just for practice, but some of the tasks include information that it might be useful to remember in any case, or that you might enjoy learning.

Making better use of your memory

It turns out that everyone has more or less the same basic memory abilities. And, in case you're wondering, no one has ever managed to "fill up" their memory so they are no longer able to remember anything further. The difference between those people with "good" memories, and the rest of us, is simply that those people have better learned to *use* their memories.

Making better use of your memory involves two basic things:

» Using your memory. If you are used to relying on technology, or written notes, then the chances are that you rarely deliberately memorize information. Luckily, even just a little practice, kept up for a couple of weeks, will lead to lasting improvements in your memory skills.

» Making use of memorization techniques. These are specific methods which you can learn to use so that day-to-day memory tasks become much more straightforward. Different techniques are relevant to different situations - so, for example, some are useful for remembering the odd thing on the spur of the moment, while others are more useful when you are making a careful effort to memorize information.

Instructions (continued)

How to use this book

You can dip into the book as you please, but you'll get the greatest benefit if you start at the beginning and work your way through in order. There are two main reasons for this:

» The book includes hints and tips information every few pages, and these will make most sense if read through in order. Some of the information, and the tips themselves, are cumulative in nature – so they will make more sense when read in the order in which they are presented.

» The memory puzzles in the book get progressively trickier and more complex as you progress, so if you jump in at the end you might be in for a bit of a shock!

Memory puzzles

The memory puzzles themselves vary considerably in terms of the skills that they will require, and the type of content you are being asked to remember. In almost all cases, however, you will be given some information and then be asked to cover it over; then you will be asked to recall that information in some way. Perhaps there will be a new list of items and you will be asked to spot differences, such as inserted items, or maybe they will have been modified or deleted. In other exercises, you are asked to recall some or all of the information you've been given. Often there are prompts to help you, but not always.

In each case, if you struggle on a puzzle then feel free to move on, but make a note of it so you can come back to it later. Perhaps you'll feel better prepared to tackle it then.

Finally, there are solutions to the Memory Sums puzzles on the last page of the book, in case you need a helping hand with the numbers. Otherwise, the solutions to the puzzles are in whatever you have been asked to remember, so are not spelled out.

Good luck, and let's get started!

Hints and Tips

Memory Training

» Your memory is a key part of you being who you are. Without it you wouldn't know what you had done, what you were planning to do – and you wouldn't even know who you were. Everything you think and feel is based on your experiences to date, and all of these are stored in your memory.

» The better you are at remembering what has happened to you, the more you gain useful experience on which to make future decisions. It's also nice to be able to have a broad range of knowledge to hand, so we can have informed and meaningful conversations, and make good sense of the media we consume.

» Perhaps you feel that your memory isn't as good as other people's, but the truth is that we all have more or less the same innate capacity. Indeed, it seems that there is no practical limit on the amount of information you can remember. What varies between people, however, is how well they *use* their memories.

» One of the most fundamental aspects of forming a memory is that we must be paying attention. Usually this means consciously noticing what we want to remember, so one of the most basic memorization tips is simply to focus on what it is that you want to remember. Being distracted or bored makes your brain think something is unimportant to remember.

» There are various techniques that can be used to make it easier to remember and then recall things, so as you progress through the book it is a good idea to start to make a conscious effort to use the memory techniques that are described. They may take some considerable effort to start with, but like many things they become easier with practice. Eventually some of these techniques will become second nature, and you will be able to enjoy the many benefits of being able to make better deliberate use of your memory.

Spot the Difference

Start with this image-based memory test. Cover over the bottom half of this page, and study the top half for up to 30 seconds. When the time is up, cover over the top half instead and follow the instructions below.

Can you circle the images that have *changed*, relative to the set of images above? When you are done, reveal the images above and see how you did.

Spot the Difference Again

If you've completed the task on the previous page, you might find it easier a second time – now that you know what to expect! Once again, cover over the bottom half of this page, and study the top half for up to 30 seconds. When the time is up, cover over the top half instead and follow the instructions below.

Can you circle the images that have *changed*, relative to the set of images above? When you are done, reveal the images above and see how you did.

Word Order

Here's another exercise, using words instead of images. Cover over the bottom half of this page, then take 30 seconds to study the music genres below. Try to memorize the *order* that they appear in. When the time is up, reveal the bottom half of the page and cover the top half instead.

1: Country

2: Electronic

3: Blues

4: Classical

5: Dance

6: Reggae

7: Hip-hop

8: Jazz

Using your memory, see if you can number the words below from 1 to 8, according to the order they were given in above:

8 Jazz 8

4 Blues 3

3 Dance 5

0 Reggae

1 Country

4 Hip-hop 7

5 Classical 4

2 Electronic

The Solar System

Read the following list of facts about our solar system, and then try the questions on the opposite page *without* referring back to the text below.

- Venus is the hottest planet in the solar system, with an average surface temperature of 426°C (863°F).

- Halley's Comet has an elliptical orbit with a period of 75–76 years. It will not return to the inner solar system until 2061.

- Ceres is the largest-known object in the asteroid belt that lies between Mars and Jupiter, with an average diameter of 946km.

- The Sun is so heavy that its mass accounts for about 99.86% of all the mass in the solar system.

- A dwarf planet is an object that orbits the sun like a planet, but which is not massive enough to have cleared its orbit of other material.

- Five objects have been classified as dwarf planets. They are Pluto, Ceres, Haumea, Makemake and Eris.

- Jupiter, Saturn, Uranus and Neptune are all gas planets but, due to their different compositions, Jupiter and Saturn are classified as gas giants, while Uranus and Neptune are classified as ice giants.

- Although Mars is a red planet, the fine dust in the atmosphere gives its sunsets a blue hue.

Solar System (continued)

Make sure you've read the opposite page first. Now, test your memory by seeing how many of the following questions you can answer:

1. Name any three of the five dwarf planets.

   Pluto, Ceres, Makemake

2. What is the average diameter of the largest known object in the asteroid belt between Mars and Jupiter?

   _948 940km_

3. Which two planets are known as ice giants?

   Neptune, Uranus

4. When will Halley's Comet next return to the inner solar system?

   _2061_

5. What does the sunset on Mars look like?

   blue hued

6. What percentage of the solar system does the Sun's mass take up?

   _99.86%_

Now go back and reread the facts again. How did you do?

You could also erase or conceal any answers you have written in, and try the same questions in an hour – or a day, or a week – and see how you do then.

Kitchen Equipment

Cover over the opposite page, then take as much time as you feel you need to remember the following images of different kitchen utensils and appliances. Once you feel that you are sufficiently familiar with the pictures, cover over this page and continue with the puzzle on the next page.

Kitchen Equipment (continued)

Make sure you have read and followed the instructions on the opposite page first, then cover it over and reveal the content below.

It's time to find out how good your visual memory is! By looking at the pictures below, can you identify the four images that have been replaced?

Hints and Tips

Short-term Memory

» You have both "short-term" and "long-term" memories. Long-term memory refers to any memory that lasts beyond around 30 seconds, whereas short-term memory refers purely to the brief memories that are gone, sometimes in seconds, unless you consciously make an effort to keep refreshing them. Imagine that you have just been given a phone number – you may hold it in your short-term memory while you write it down. Even then you may forget it, unless you keep rehearsing the memory to stop it fading from your short-term memory.

» Attempting to write down a phone number reveals another feature of short-term memory, namely that you can only remember around five to eight individual items at any one time. As you attempt to remember a later one, you forget a previous one. The extent of your short-term memory is essentially fixed, although you can learn to use it more effectively by representing memories more compactly – e.g. you might remember "2" and "0" as a single item, "20".

» Most short-term memories are never transferred to long-term memory – which is lucky, since otherwise our memories would be filled with mostly useless information. If you don't pay close attention to something, it will more than likely not be transferred to your brain's long-term memory.

» It is likely that you have different short-term memories for each of your senses. This means, for example, that remembering smells, sounds and sights does not interfere with your ability to remember words and numbers.

Memory Sums

This page contains two separate puzzles, divided by a line.

For each puzzle, start by covering over the second row of numbers. Then, study the top set of three numbers for just five seconds.

When five seconds are up, cover the first row and simultaneously uncover the second row. Using just your memory to recall the original numbers, which of the new numbers in the second row can be formed by *adding* together two of the numbers from the first row?

Once you have decided, check back to the original numbers. Were you right?

Next, repeat with the second puzzle on the page.

Row 1 – numbers:

3   5   8

Row 2 – totals to form:

7   9   (11)

Row 1 – numbers:

13   17   22

Row 2 – totals to form:

31   35   (39)

Turn to the final page of the book to check the solutions.

Band Positions

By paying careful attention, see if you can memorize whereabouts on the page each of the following band names have been printed. Don't worry about memorizing the full names accurately, but rather just focus on where each band is located.

The Rolling Stones

Coldplay

The Beatles

Foo Fighters

Green Day

Beastie Boys

Muse

Fall Out Boy

Now, cover over the bands above and see if you can place each band back in its original location on the page. The bands were:

The Rolling Stones, The Beatles, Fall Out Boy, Muse, Foo Fighters, Green Day, Beastie Boys and Coldplay

TRS

Coldplay

Beatles

FF

Green Day

BB

Muse

FOB

European Rivers

Have a look at the list of eight European rivers below. Try to remember as many as you can over the next 60 seconds.

Rhine

Danube

Seine

Elbe

Loire

Moselle

Thames

Volga

Now, cover over the rivers above and see if you can recall them all. Write them out on the lines below:

_____   _____

_____   _____

_____   _____

_____   _____

The Interview

Read the story below carefully, then, once you are familiar with the text, cover it up and try to answer the questions on the opposite page.

Officer Davis looked annoyed. No, worse than just annoyed, Marcus realized. She looked positively fuming. Her thick, dark eyebrows were knitted together in a frown, and her tight, unsmiling lips seemed even more tightly pinched as she looked over the notes once more. "Tell me again, Mister Atkins, what you did on the morning of the 14th of January?"

"We've been through this!" said Marcus, exasperatedly, and he glanced with desperation towards his suited solicitor. "What do you need me to say?"

Officer Davis sat up. "I need you to talk me through everything that happened that morning."

Marcus nodded, pushing his glasses up his nose again and placing his palms flat on the table. "I woke up at 7.45, just like I always do. I got up, went to the bathroom." He eyed her, expecting a reaction but receiving only a stony-faced gaze. "Then I went for a run for an hour, on my own. Stoney Park, along the mud track by the river."

"What were you wearing?"

He wrinkled his nose a little. "A grey hoodie, red shorts. These white kicks." He gestured to his feet. "It was raining," he added, in case the detail might help. Officer Davis glanced down to his proffered foot.

"They look pretty clean for having run in the mud," she snapped suspiciously. "I think you're lying."

The Interview (continued)

Have you read the story on the opposite page? If not, read that page first before returning to this one.

Now you have read the story, see if you can answer the questions below. Don't check back – try and answer them using just your memory.

1. In what way are Officer Davis' eyebrows described?

   _____

2. What is Marcus' surname?

   _____

3. What was the date of the events Officer Davis wanted to discuss?

   _____

4. What time did Marcus claim to have woken up?

   _____

5. What was the name of the park Marcus had run in?

   _____

6. What clothes did Marcus claim to have been wearing for his run?

   _____

How did you do? If there were any you couldn't answer, read the piece again and give it another go.

Camping Expedition

Start by covering over the opposite page.

Below are nine pictures of things you might see or bring on a camping expedition. On the opposite page are the same pictures, but in a different order. Study the images below for up to 30 seconds, and try to memorize the order they are arranged in. Then cover them over and reveal the page opposite.

Camping Expedition (continued)

Make sure you have completed and covered over the previous page first.

Now, can you draw lines to attach each image to the position it originally occupied on the previous page? For example, if you think the top-left image was previously arranged in the middle of the middle row, then draw a line from the top-left image to the middle box on the middle row.

Hints and Tips

» There is no limit on long-term memory, so in theory you could remember as much as you ever wanted to. However, in practice we all inevitably forget things that we want to recall, and even those things we do successfully remember start to fade over time.

» Much of what we remember, we have learned without making any conscious effort to do so. However, if you keep forgetting things that you had hoped to remember, there are various techniques you can consciously make use of to help you learn. For example, to help remember what you read, you could try reading it out loud as well as just reading it silently, or listen to an audiobook as well – consuming the same information in multiple ways helps make it more memorable.

» Even if you have successfully learned something, you may still have trouble recalling it. In such cases, try to think of related information that might act as a trigger to the information you want to recall. For example, think about where you were when you learned it, or what you might have learned alongside it.

» It's easier to *recognize* something that you have seen before than it is to retrieve it without a cue. You would therefore find it significantly harder to list 100 books that you have read than to identify 100 books you have read from a list that is given to you.

» It's worth noting that even very specific knowledge you have successfully learned, such as detailed mathematical equations or the formulae of chemical compounds, will slowly be forgotten if it is never used. In order to retain these memories, they or their related memories need to be regularly used.

Movie Memory

As you tackle this memory puzzle, you'll be using your long-term memory. Begin by covering over the bottom half of the page, then study this list of Oscar winners for Best Director for 30–40 seconds. Next, cover them over and reveal the bottom half of the page. In the recall part of this puzzle, you will then be given *either* the director *or* the movie title as a prompt. The year of the ceremony where each award was given is listed in both halves of the puzzle.

- 1951: George Stevens, *A Place in the Sun*

- 1965: Robert Wise, *The Sound of Music*

- 1978: Michael Cimino, *The Deer Hunter*

- 1985: Sydney Pollack, *Out of Africa*

- 1999: Sam Mendes, *American Beauty*

Now see if you can fill in the missing information, when prompted by the director or the title. How many of these Oscar-winning directors or their movies can you recall?

- 1951: _____, directed by George Stevens

- 1965: *The Sound of Music*, directed by _____

- 1978: *The Deer Hunter*, directed by _____

- 1985: _____, directed by Sydney Pollack

- 1999: _____, directed by Sam Mendes

Pictures and Words

Start by covering over the bottom half of the page, then notice how each of the six images below has a word next to it. Take some time to study the pictures and words, making an effort to remember which word is associated with which picture. Once you think you have learned the associations, cover them up instead and continue reading below.

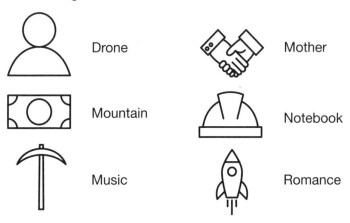

Written below are the six words that were given at the top of the page. Can you now draw lines to join each word to the same image that it was originally next to?

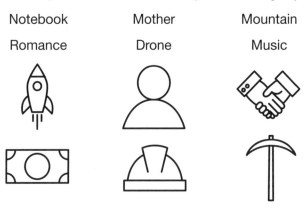

Connections Challenge

Sometimes you can use ridiculous or humorous connections to make something mundane much more memorable. Consider the ten items in the shopping list in the left column below, for example. Taken on their own, they might be hard to memorize, but if you try linking them in amusing ways it can get easier – then you just need to remember the first item, since the connections will be recalled more easily.

For example, starting from **milk**, it could be pouring into a giant bowl of **cereal**, which is being eaten by a living **can opener**, which is busy cutting **string** into pieces, and so on. The sillier the connections, the easier it will be to remember the list.

Write your own ideas for connections to the next item in the space to the right of each item:

Milk	_____
Cereal	_____
Can opener	_____
String	_____
Chocolate	_____
Frying pan	_____
Lemons	_____
Custard	_____
Mustard	_____
Cheese	_____

When you have finished creating associations for each word, read over them to remind yourself of them, then cover the words. Now, how many of the items can you recall by starting from the first word: **Milk**

Something Fishy

Cover over the bottom half of the page, then look at the list of aquarium fish below. After 60 seconds, cover them over and then look at the list at the bottom half of the page. Which fish are missing from the second list?

Catfish

Tetra

Gourami

Goldfish

Cichlid

Darter

Squeaker

Corydoras

Now cover the above list and look at the one below, which has been reordered. Can you say which three fish are missing from this list?

Catfish

Cichlid

Corydoras

Gourami

Squeaker

Elemental Exercise

It can be tricky to remember which chemical element symbol expands into which element. For example, is "Ag" the symbol for gold or for silver? One way to help make this kind of thing more memorable is to look to create easy-to-remember links. For example, as a child you might have been taught to remember the spelling of "separate" by being told "there's 'a rat' in sep<u>arat</u>e".

Here are some symbols and their associated elements. Can you invent some aide-memoires to help you recall which is which? The first one is done for you as an example of how this might work, although of course there is no single right answer for any of them.

1. Gold (Au)

    Remember it as "**Gau**ld" to help recall that it is "au", not "ag"

2. Silver (Ag)

    _____

3. Sodium (Na)

    _____

4. Tin (Sn)

    _____

5. Iron (Fe)

    _____

6. Tungsten (W)

    _____

Hints and Tips

» "Procedural" memory refers to all of those long-term memories which permit us to perform tasks that we can do without consciously thinking about – such as eating, walking or writing.

» With practice, we usually get better at any skill. This is because our procedural memory is improving, as we learn to dedicate less conscious effort to each individual muscle movement we make. For example, when you first learn to drive you need to consciously think about each movement of your hands or feet, especially for a manual car, whereas with some practice you stop needing to concentrate on each individual movement and can focus instead on improving your road skills.

» With enough practice we are able to perform some physical actions without conscious thought. Walking is an obvious example, but as a further example a professional sports player's procedural memory of their game will be so advanced that they will be able to play without thinking about much more than the tactics they wish to employ – whereas a beginner might need to concentrate on every racket swing or ball kick, for example.

» If you want to improve a physical skill, the first step is to remember to focus when you are learning. For example, if you are learning to play golf you shouldn't swing blindly. Think about your grip on the club, your stance and how you swing your body through to hit the ball. Like learning to walk, it can be a slow and painful process to begin with.

» For many physical skills, such as dancing, you can learn the skill faster just by *thinking* about making the appropriate physical movements. This can be helpful when you don't have sufficient opportunity for physical practice. Your brain will gently tense the correct muscles at the correct times as you envision the movements, so it can even contribute to staying fit!

Just Juggling

Some physical skills can take a long time to learn, and it is sometimes claimed that it can take 10,000 hours to master an activity – but of course this depends on both the activity and your natural aptitude for it. It certainly takes a long time – and a great innate ability – to become a concert pianist, but most people can learn to do basic juggling in less than a week.

This exercise will refer to juggling three balls, but you can apply similar techniques to the learning of any physical skill.

Say that you want to learn to juggle. You could split your time over a week like this:

Step 1

Take just one ball, and throw it directly up in a vertical line from your dominant hand, then catch it in the same hand. Repeat until you can do this without having to regularly move around to catch it. Ideally you will be able to do so without moving your feet or body at all, beyond your arm. Once this is mastered, repeat with the other arm. You can also mix up using each arm, to keep things interesting.

Step 2

Now you can catch a ball in the same hand without moving, repeat Step 1 but catch the ball in the *other* hand. Throw the ball in an arc now, instead of throwing straight up. Your aim should be to be able to throw perfectly to the other hand without significantly moving your body, other than your arms, at all. Repeat throwing from the other hand too.

The higher you can throw the ball and still be able to catch it most of the time in the other hand, the easier you will find it when you move to the next step.

Step 3

Now you will need two balls. Hold one ball in each hand, and then repeat Step 2 while throwing from *both* hands. To be precise, throw from your dominant hand to your other hand, and then – while the ball is in the air – throw from your other hand to your dominant hand. Repeat until you can confidently catch a ball in both hands without moving much.

Step 4

You're nearly there! Now you just need to hold two balls in your dominant hand, and time your throws so you can get all three balls in the air at once – and then as you catch one ball, throw it back to the other hand again.

Names and Faces

Cover over the part of this page beneath the faces, then spend as long as you feel you need attempting to memorize the names of each of the following people. Next, cover over the names and faces and reveal the question at the bottom of the page.

Jennifer	Sanjit	Harriet

Brian	Seeta	Noah

Which of the following people were featured on this page, and which did not appear? Circle or cross them out as appropriate.

Seeta	**Norman**	**Brian**
Harry	**Jane**	**Susan**

Now check your answer. How did you do?

Names and Faces (continued)

To solve this puzzle, first complete the puzzle on the opposite page. Then, cover over the entirety of the opposite page before continuing.

Do you still remember the faces? Time to find out!

Which of the following people did you see on the previous page? Cross out the people who are new, but **write the name** of the person underneath those that you have seen before.

Farmer Fred

Read the story below carefully. Once you are familiar with the text, cover it over and try to answer the questions on the opposite page.

Farmer Fred was a jolly old man, with bright blue eyes and a big, beaming smile. He had lived at Pipplesqueak Farm since the day he was born, many moons back. Over the years, his family at the Farm had grown. He had married Felicity Jackson, and they now had three lovely children, named Fillip, Florence and Francis.

Each morning, Farmer Fred woke at the crack of dawn as the cockerel crowed, and pulled on his boots to trundle out to the yard. He did the same no matter the time of year or weather, since he made sure to check on all of his animals on each and every day.

To make sure he never missed anyone, he visited all of his animals in the same order every day. He would start with the pigs, and then move on to the goats. The sheep were next, then the horses, and then the cows. Finally, he would always end his rounds with a trip to the chickens, where he would check to see how many eggs there were for breakfast.

When he returned to the farmhouse after his animal rounds each morning, he would give his wife Felicity a kiss on the nose, and declare they should have eggs for breakfast again. Farmer Fred was a very happy man.

Farmer Fred (continued)

Have you read the story on the previous page? If not, go back and read it before returning to this page.

Once you have familiarized yourself with the text, see if you can answer the following questions *without* checking back to the opposite page.

1. How is Farmer Fred's appearance described?

   _____

2. What is the name of Farmer Fred's farm?

   _____

3. What are the names of his three children?

   _____

4. Farmer Fred always visited his goats, cows, chickens and pigs. What other two types of animal did he visit?

   _____

5. Can you remember the exact order that Farmer Fred visited the animals in?

   _____

6. What did Farmer Fred do on returning to the farmhouse every day, before suggesting eggs for breakfast?

   _____

How did you get on? If there were any questions you weren't sure about, reread the story and try again.

Hints and Tips

Repetition

» If you encounter something only once it will most likely fade from your memory quite quickly, unless it's very memorable. Go over successfully memorized information soon after you've learnt it in order to reinforce the memories and make them last longer.

» Repeatedly rehearse information not just as you learn it, but also an hour later, a day later, a week later, and even a month later, if you wish the memories to be long-lasting.

» When you are going over information, make a note of the parts you tend to forget so you can make a special effort to review and remember them.

» Repetition won't work so well if you aren't paying proper attention, which can be an issue when you go over the same information time and again, so try to add variety by repeating the information in different forms. For example, you could read different books or articles on the same subject, or find a talk or documentary that covers the same material. You could also try visualizing information, perhaps with diagrams – or by picturing events taking place if appropriate.

» Summarize and reformat information, for example by taking notes and then rehearsing from those notes. Another useful method is to write questions for yourself, and then see if you can still successfully answer those questions when you return at a later time or date.

Poetry Poser

There are some things that it is almost impossible to memorize without repetition.

Try learning this classic poem, as well as you can. You will probably need to repeat it many times, perhaps breaking it down by line, until you can recall it all without effort.

If you struggle, you might also try remembering just the first word of each line. This word might prompt you to recall the rest of the line when you are more familiar with the poem.

Sonnet VII – by John Keats, 1795–1821

O Solitude! if I must with thee dwell,

Let it not be among the jumbled heap

Of murky buildings; climb with me the steep, –

Nature's observatory – whence the dell,

Its flowery slopes, its river's crystal swell,

May seem a span; let me thy vigils keep

'Mongst boughs pavillion'd, where the deer's swift leap

Startles the wild bee from the fox-glove bell.

But though I'll gladly trace these scenes with thee,

Yet the sweet converse of an innocent mind,

Whose words are images of thoughts refin'd,

Is my soul's pleasure; and it sure must be

Almost the highest bliss of human-kind,

When to thy haunts two kindred spirits flee.

PINs and Passwords

Most of us need to recall passwords and PIN codes on a daily basis, but unfortunately we tend to reuse the same passwords and codes – which lessens the security.

One way to simplify learning a new password or PIN is to connect it either to yourself or the account in some way, and then (in the case of a password) to combine it with a password from a much smaller set you have memorized. For example, you could make a web password more secure by adding an abbreviated version of the name of the site to one of a small set of genuinely memorized passwords. In this way, should the password be compromised then it cannot be directly used on another site. Or, for PINs, you could construct them from numbers and dates that have meaning to you.

See how easily you can learn the following pretend passwords and PINs. Spend a few moments focusing on these, and then cover them over and see if you can recall them from the prompts below.

Bank of Imagination: boiMypass3

Bank PIN: 9756

Gym locker: C1470A

Computer login: compMypass1

When you think you are ready, cover over the above and see if you can recall all of the passwords and PINs:

Bank PIN _____

Computer login _____

Gym locker _____

Bank of Imagination _____

Famous Mountains

Have a look at the list of ten mountains below. Try to remember as many as you can in the next 60 seconds, then see how many you recall below when just given the initials of their names.

Ben Nevis

Chimborazo

Denali

Elbrus

Everest

Kilimanjaro

Lhotse

Logan

Rainier

Snowdon

Now, cover over the mountains above. How many can you recall, given the initials below?

B_____ N_____   C_____

C_____   E_____

E_____   K_____

L_____   L_____

R_____   S_____

Image Array

Cover over the opposite page.

Now, look at the following 16 pictures. Spend as long as you feel you need memorizing them. Then, cover them over and turn to the next page where you will be asked to identify which images are missing.

Image Array (continued)

Start by reading the opposite page. If you have already done so, then make sure the opposite page is covered and continue reading.

There were 16 pictures on the previous page, but there are only 12 on this one. Can you recall and then write down descriptions of the four items that are now missing? Or, if you prefer, then feel free to make a drawing of them instead in the space provided.

Hints and Tips

Acronyms and Abbreviations

» One technique to help you memorize short sets or small chunks of information is to encapsulate them using acronyms or abbreviations. The aim here is to shrink multiple pieces of information into one smaller item, which is intrinsically easier to remember. So long as you have enough familiarity with the original items that you can recall them from the smaller trigger item, then this can be a very effective method.

» Acronyms take the first letters of words and link them together. A classic example of an acronym memory aid is to use ROYGBIV to help you remember that the rainbow is ordered Red, Orange, Yellow, Green, Blue, Indigo and Violet. Although it is a bit of a strange 'word', it is much easier to remember this two-syllable word than the exact order of the seven hues.

» Acronyms work because your brain retrieves words based on their first letter, which means that using an acronym or abbreviation to prompt you with the first letter of a word is often enough to help you recall the rest – especially if you know the items already, but just need to learn their ordering.

» When using an acronym as a memory tool, it may not be easily pronounceable which will in turn make it harder to remember. Therefore it can be better to use an acronym-like abbreviation, where you add in extra letters to facilitate being able to more easily say – and therefore memorize – it. Of course, you do then need to remember which letters are and aren't important in the resulting memory aid.

» You can be creative with abbreviation memory aids, so long as they make sense to you. For example, you may want to remember that Lisbon is the capital of Portugal by using the abbreviation 'LisP'.

State Capitals

Form abbreviations in this next task by writing an abbreviation-based memory prompt that links each American state with its capital. Although these may not always help you, they at least *increase* the likelihood that you can remember which capital goes with which state.

For example, you might use **HiHon** (pronounced, perhaps, as 'Hi, hon!' to link Hawaii (which has the postal abbreviation HI) and its capital Honolulu.

Six more state capitals are given below, along with their state and its postal abbreviation. Can you come up with clever ways to help remind yourself in future (or learn in the first place) which capital belongs to which state?

1. Montgomery, Alabama (AL)

_____

2. Sacramento, California (CA)

_____

3. Tallahassee, Florida (FL)

_____

4. Albany, New York (NY)

_____

5. Columbus, Ohio (OH)

_____

6. Richmond, Virginia (VA)

_____

Presidential Abbreviations

See if you can come up with an abbreviation or acronym-based technique to help you (or someone else, if you already know them) to learn the order that these ten US presidents served in.

31st: Herbert Hoover

32nd: Franklin D. Roosevelt

33rd: Harry S. Truman

34th: Dwight D. Eisenhower

35th: John F. Kennedy

36th: Lyndon B. Johnson

37th: Richard Nixon

38th: Gerald Ford

39th: Jimmy Carter

40th: Ronald Reagan

Use these lines to make notes, or to write out your finished memory aid:

_____

_____

_____

_____

When you have finished creating your abbreviation, make a note of it elsewhere and then see if you can use it to prompt yourself at a later date. You could also test yourself to see if you can remember the abbreviation itself, and then if you can retrieve the presidents from it.

Gemstones

Have a look at the list of 12 gemstones below. Using any technique you like, study them for 60 seconds before covering them over. Then, see if you can recall them in the area given at the bottom of the page. You might like to use an abbreviation-based technique to help you remember the first letters of the gemstones, to use as a prompt.

Amethyst

Aquamarine

Diamond

Emerald

Garnet

Opal

Pearl

Ruby

Sapphire

Topaz

Tourmaline

Turquoise

_____   _____

_____   _____

_____   _____

_____   _____

_____   _____

_____   _____

Fruit and Vegetables

Start by covering over the opposite page.

Below are nine pictures of fruit and vegetables. On the opposite page are the same pictures, but in a different order. Study the images below for up to 30 seconds, and try to memorize the order they are arranged in. Then cover them over and reveal the page opposite.

Fruit and Vegetables (continued)

Make sure you have completed and covered over the previous page first.

Now, can you draw lines to attach each image to the position it originally occupied on the previous page? For example, if you think the top-left image was previously arranged in the middle of the middle row, then draw a line from the top-left image to the middle box on the middle row.

Hints and Tips

Acrostics

» We saw a few pages back how acronyms and abbreviations can be used to help you learn the order of small sets of information, or as a memory prompt to help you recall a set of items. However, abbreviations and acronyms become ineffective for longer sequences – but can be replaced with acrostics instead.

» Just as abbreviations and acronyms remind you of initial letters in a given order, so acrostics work in the same way by using alternative words that start with the same letters – but instead of a string of standalone items or facts, you search for a memorable phrase or sentence that uses them instead. For example, you could remember the order of the planets, and prompt yourself with the initial letters of their names, by using the sentence, 'My Very Educated Mother Just Served Us Noodles.' Notice how the initial letters of these words correspond with Mercury, Venus, Earth, Mars, Jupiter, Saturn, Uranus and Neptune.

» You can be flexible and creative when creating acrostics. You could for example allow prepositions or conjunctions, such as "the" and "and", to be included but not form part of the acrostic initial sequence. This could make it much easier to find suitable acrostics. Of course, you do have to then remember the rules you are using!

» Acrostics can be very effective, especially if you are flexible with how you use them. You could even create an acrostic poem, where the first letter of each *line*, rather than word, creates the acrostic.

World Cup Initials

As the final tip opposite mentions, the acrostic technique isn't limited to sentences. See if you can write an acrostic poem to help you remember the order of the eight most recent winners of the FIFA Soccer World Cup (as of 2019), which were as shown below. A line is given below each country for you to insert the appropriate line of the poem. Note that this is simply an exercise, and there is no need to learn the resulting poem – unless you want to!

1. 1990: Germany

    _____

2. 1994: Brazil

    _____

3. 1998: France

    _____

4. 2002: Brazil

    _____

5. 2006: Italy

    _____

6. 2010: Spain

    _____

7. 2014: Germany

    _____

8. 2018: France

    _____

Evening Romance

Read the story below carefully. Then, when you feel are sufficiently familiar with the text, answer the questions on the opposite page.

The fire burned on the beach, crackling and sending bright little sparks of ash up into the air as the flames licked hungrily around the wood. There was the perfect breeze blowing, pushing the loose strands of Ella's hair back and away from her face as she stared out at the sun setting on the horizon.

"Are you cold?" Josh asked gently, dropping his warm, blue jacket onto her shoulders. The palm of his hand rested on her upper back for a moment before rubbing in a gentle circular motion over her shoulder blade, making her shiver.

"You're welcome to warm me up," she suggested with a small, shy smile, peeking up at him through her long eyelashes. Josh's lips broke into that glorious, boyish smile of his and he nodded, sinking down onto the sand beside her and wrapping one arm around her, tugging her in a little closer. His head rested on her shoulder as his hand ran down her arm, finding her fingers to entwine with his own.

For a few moments, they simply enjoyed listening to the gentle crash of the waves on the shore, before Josh's hand tightened around Ella's with a playful squeeze. "Come on," he encouraged, clambering to his feet and pulling her to follow him. "Let's dip our toes in the water before it gets too dark."

Evening Romance (continued)

Did you read the story on the previous page? If not, go back and have a look before returning to this page. Cover it over before continuing.

Now that you've read the text, see if you can answer the questions below.

1. Where are the couple located?

2. What time of day is it?

3. How is Josh's smile described?

4. What item of clothing does Josh give to Ella?

5. What sounds can the couple hear on the beach?

6. What is Josh said to "encourage" Ella to do?

Could you answer all the questions? If not, go back and read the article again – before covering it over and trying again.

A Simple Thai

Read and attempt to memorize the recipe below. Then, cover it over and complete as much of the original recipe information on the following page as possible. There are a few prompts to help you, but you'll still need to be paying attention!

Peel and finely chop an inch of ginger, two cloves of garlic and one large, white onion. Lightly saute in oil in a wok.

Slice two chicken breasts into small pieces, and add to the wok for ten minutes, turning regularly.

Chop one sweet pepper, one Chinese cabbage and a handful of Brussels sprouts into strips, then add to the wok.

Add one heaped spoonful of red Thai curry paste, followed by one can of coconut milk, to the wok, then simmer for 30 minutes.

Wash one cupful of rice, then add to a separate pan with two cupfuls of cold water. Bring to the boil and then put a lid on the pan. Simmer for 20 minutes.

Check the chicken is cooked and no longer pink in the middle.

Serve chicken and rice together with a squeeze of lime.

A Simple Thai (continued)

Did you read the recipe on the opposite page? If not, go back and read it now before returning to this page – and cover over the opposite page.

Once you have memorized the recipe, see how many of the missing words below you can fill in.

Peel and finely chop an _____ of ginger, _____ cloves of garlic and one large, _____ _____. Lightly saute in oil in a wok.

Slice two _____ _____ into small pieces, and add to the wok for _____ minutes, turning regularly.

Chop one _____ _____, one Chinese cabbage and a handful of Brussels sprouts into strips, then add to the wok.

Add one heaped spoonful of red Thai curry paste, followed by one can of _____ _____, to the wok, then _____ for _____ minutes.

Wash one cupful of rice, then add to a separate pan with _____ cupfuls of cold water. Bring to the boil and then put a lid on the pan. Simmer for _____ minutes.

Check the chicken is cooked and no longer pink in the middle.

Serve chicken and rice together with a _____ _____ _____.

Hints and Tips

Writing it Down

» Repetition is one of the keys to effective learning, and one good way to force yourself to repeat information is to write it down.

» Simply writing something out verbatim is one option, but summarizing information into notes is even more effective because to be able to form notes you must be paying attention.

» When you write notes, try to present the information differently in some way, perhaps by paraphrasing or rearranging material slightly, so that you need to form a deeper understanding of the material as you go. This will make it more memorable.

» Once you've finished writing notes, you can further repeat the material by organizing the notes into sections. This process of summarizing and organizing information takes focus, which ensures that you will be paying attention and helps to make the material more memorable. Otherwise, by the third time you look at the material, you may not be paying as much attention.

» To add to the repetition and even give yourself a brain training exercise, you can then edit your notes down when you are done. The need to more deeply understand your material, as well as the chance to excise material you are now properly familiar with, will make your brain – and therefore memory – pay attention all over again.

» You can also try transferring your notes across media, for example by dictating them into a microphone, or simply reading and explaining them to someone else.

» Another way of writing notes is to summarize them into prompt questions, which can also focus future learning on areas where you have the most trouble.

Directions

Can you memorize these directions? If it helps, you could make some written notes on the ruled lines below, or maybe draw a brief diagram in the space given.

To get to the museum, walk one mile in the direction of the Old Town Square. When you reach it, take the first left and then take the following right. Walk six blocks, past the farm on your left, and take a sharp right by the Giant Lobster statue. Walk about half a mile through the field until you reach the Museum of Moos.

Use this area to make written notes:

_____

_____

_____

_____

Or you could draw a diagram here:

Now cover over the page, and see if you can recall the route.

Jane Eyre

Below are the opening lines from the novel *Jane Eyre*, written by Charlotte Brontë.

Test your memory skills by reading it through carefully, taking each word into consideration – but without rereading it. Then, when you have finished the passage, cover it over and read the instructions at the top of the opposite page.

There was no possibility of taking a walk that day. We had been wandering, indeed, in the leafless shrubbery an hour in the morning; but since dinner (Mrs Reed, when there was no company, dined early) the cold winter wind had brought with it clouds so sombre, and a rain so penetrating, that further out-door exercise was now out of the question.

I was glad of it: I never liked long walks, especially on chilly afternoons: dreadful to me was the coming home in the raw twilight, with nipped fingers and toes, and a heart saddened by the chidings of Bessie, the nurse, and humbled by the consciousness of my physical inferiority to Eliza, John, and Georgiana Reed.

Jane Eyre (continued)

Start on the opposite page, if you have not yet completed the exercise there.

Making sure that you have covered over the text on the opposite page, read through the copy of it below. Ten words have been changed. Can you underline or circle them all? To help you, five are in the first paragraph, and five in the second.

There was no possibility of taking a stroll that day. We had been wandering, indeed, in the barren shrubbery an hour in the morning; but since lunch (Mrs Reed, when there was no company, dined early) the cold spring wind had brought with it clouds so sombre, and a rain so penetrating, that continued out-door exercise was now out of the question.

I was glad of it: I never liked long walks, particularly on chilly afternoons: unwelcome to me was the coming home in the raw twilight, with chapped fingers and toes, and a soul saddened by the chidings of Bessie, the nurse, and humbled by the consciousness of my tangible inferiority to Eliza, John, and Georgiana Reed.

Norse Gods

Take 60 seconds to focus on these different Norse Gods, then cover them over and see how many you can recall when prompted with the first letter of each of the names.

Bragi

Thor

Njord

Odin

Balder

Aegir

Vali

Freya

Einherjar

Forseti

Now cover over the list and see if you can recall them all.

B_____   T_____

N_____   O_____

B_____   A_____

V_____   F_____

E_____   F_____

Shades of Paint

Cover over the bottom list on this page, and then take a look at the eight shades of paint listed immediately below. When you are sufficiently familiar with them, cover them over and continue reading halfway down the page.

Aquamarine

Turquoise

Peacock

Blue

Jade

Green

Cobalt

Emerald

Now cover the top half of the page and read the following list. Can you work out which paints are missing, and add them to the end of the list? Also, can you cross out the paints that have been inserted and which were not originally included?

Cerulean	Cream
Blue	Emerald
Turquoise	Aquamarine
Jade	Peacock
Red	Sky
_____	_____

Hints and Tips

Rhyme and Rhythm

» Have you ever noticed how song lyrics can get stuck in your head (along with their tunes, sometimes!), and yet you might struggle to remember far more useful things? This is because things that have a rhythm or rhyme to them are intrinsically far easier to remember. Perhaps our brains pay attention to the patterns and think that they might be important to remember.

» Given that it is much easier to remember sentences or phrases that rhyme or have a good rhythm, we can use this fact to help make material more memorable. Combine rhythm *and* rhyme and you make something even easier to recall, such as the famous rhyming couplet "In fourteen hundred and ninety-two, Columbus sailed the ocean blue."

» Rhythm is particularly useful for cueing sentence structure and therefore the number of words. This is one reason why poems are easier to remember than basic prose, because the rhythm acts as a memory trigger.

» A way to use rhyme and rhythm to help you memorize and recall information is, of course, to write your own rhyming poems or rhyming phrases. They don't need to make a great deal of sense – think of it as an excuse to be creative! And, if you struggle to rhyme certain sentences or pieces of information, then focus on the rhythm instead, or "cheat" with partial rhymes. You could even add a tune, if you really want to commit it to memory!

» You can also take advantage of existing tunes and lyrics from songs that you like. Simply replace the lyrics with the information you're trying to memorize, even perhaps keeping some of the existing lyrics if this helps you.

Rhyming Schedule

Can you write a rhyming poem to help you remember the schedule below?

- 10.00   Doctor appointment about migraines

- 11.00   Buy eggs and bread

- 1.00   Pick up Matt's present from the gift shop

- 4.00   Matt's birthday party at Dave's house

Your poem might include time prompts, notes about what you need to do or the places you need to go to. Write the rhyme out, then read it a few times to help you remember it.

_____

_____

_____

_____

Tomorrow, come back to this page and cover over the schedule above. Can you answer these questions about your schedule?

1. What time is your appointment with the doctor?

_____

2. Where is Matt's birthday party?

_____

3. What food did you need to buy?

_____

Remembering Rhymes

Read the following set of rhyming lines. Later, come back and try to recall each of the lines, in the same order, on the opposite page.

Here it is – here comes the sun.

Heavens above, this weighs a ton!

Whoopi Goldberg played a nun.

My child can count right up to one.

Attila was a famous Hun.

Who was it ate the sticky bun?

That toy soldier has a gun!

Now look what you've gone and done.

Did you enjoy my witty pun?

This was the only game I've won.

Think of all the races run.

Well, surely that was so much fun!

It might help to draw a little picture next to each line to help you visualize it, which may in turn also make it easier to recall the lines and their order later.

Remembering Rhymes (continued)

Do you remember all of those rhyming lines from the previous page? See if you can fill them all in in the original order below.

_____

_____

_____

_____

_____

_____

_____

_____

_____

_____

_____

_____

How did you do? Did you miss any out? Were the ones you did remember still in the correct order?

The Painting

Read the story below carefully and, once you are ready, cover the text over and try to answer the questions on the following page.

"I love the brushstrokes." The critic tugged at the end of his moustache as he leaned forward, peering at the elegant curls of pigment on the canvas. "You used oils here?"

He didn't wait for an answer as he continued to coo over the image, all the time running his fingertips over the hair on his upper lip. Every now and then, he would glance over at Didier with an approving look, before turning his attention back to the painting.

"This purple here is beautiful," he said, gesturing to a swirl of mauve and violet. "Not enough artists use purple in sunsets, in my opinion."

Didier bristled with pride, crossing his arms confidently. "Then not enough artists *watch* the sun set," he grinned. "It is a magical time of day, to watch the night claim control of the sky." He leaned forward, pointing to a patch of purple on the painting's horizon. "This here is Prussian blue mixed with quinacridone magenta," he explained. "I'm glad you like it."

"It's wonderful!" the critic claimed. "I think it's even better than *Sun on Spanish Water*. Tell me, will you be selling this to Mona's Gallery? Or might it be available for a private sale?"

The Painting (continued)

Have you read the story on the previous page? If not, go back and read the text before returning to this page.

Now you have read the text, try to recall the answers to these questions from your memory.

1. What type of paint did Didier use on the canvas?

   _____

2. What facial hair is the critic described as having?

   _____

3. What shades of purple are mentioned?

   _____

4. What two paints did Didier combine for the horizon?

   _____

5. What is the first thing the critic praises in the text?

   _____

6. What is the name of the painting the critic compares Didier's new painting to?

   _____

How did you do? If there were any questions you could not answer, go back and read the story again before retrying them.

Hints and Tips

» It can be extremely frustrating bumping into someone and not being able to remember their name. Or, perhaps, meeting a group of people at an event and then realizing you have forgotten all of their names within a minute of the introductions. If either of these situations are familiar to you, and you are someone that struggles to remember names, or even faces, the good news is that there are simple techniques you can try that might be able to help.

» The single most important step of remembering someone's name is simply paying attention when you are introduced. Consciously take note of their name, and take a good look at their face. Often, we don't remember a name simply because we never really tried. When someone introduces themselves, we're only half listening (often because we are thinking what we want to say ourselves) and therefore don't really take proper note of their name. Next time you meet someone new, try paying close attention for just that moment and see if it helps you remember their name.

» The human brain is very good at recognizing faces, even if it isn't always so good at recalling their associated names. One way to help with this, however, is to find a humorous connection between their appearance and their name. You can then use this to prompt you to recall the name. For example, if someone is called Penny and has a round face or big eyes, you could make the association between the name Penny and a penny coin.

» Using a nickname alliteration, where you find a word that starts with the same letters as the person's name, is a good way of creating a memorable connection. You can use both physical and personal characteristics to create these alliterations or associations. If the person's name is Felicity, then perhaps they are Friendly Felicity – and this would also work, sarcastically, if they were particularly unwelcoming too! It's best, of course, not to *tell* the person the nickname you give them, since it might offend – but it's all in a good cause from your own point of view!

An Alliteration Aliases Alice

Use an alliteration technique to help you remember these names. You may know someone with the same name which can assist you in thinking of matching characteristics. However, if you don't know anyone with the name, simply think of amusing or endearing alliterations that could be attached. Write them below each name.

For example: **Sara** could be **Smiley Sara**.

1. Felix

_____

2. Miranda

_____

3. Simon

_____

4. Julia

_____

5. Arnold

_____

6. Daisy

_____

Names and Faces

Cover over the part of this page beneath the faces, then spend as long as you feel you need attempting to memorize the names of each of the following people. Next, cover over the names and faces and reveal the question at the bottom of the page.

| Harriet | Harvey | Kaniskha |
| Kieran | Callianassa | Dave |

Which of the following people were featured on this page, and which did not appear? Circle or cross them out as appropriate.

Jane	Humphrey	Keira
Harriet	Cassie	Dave
Andrew	Henry	Jim

Now check your answer. How did you do?

Names and Faces (continued)

To solve this puzzle, first complete the puzzle on the opposite page. Then, cover over the entirety of the opposite page before continuing.

Do you still remember the faces? Time to find out!

Which of the following people did you see on the previous page? Cross out the people who are new, but **write the name** of the person underneath those that you have seen before.

PINs and Passwords

Most of us need to recall passwords and PIN codes on a daily basis, but unfortunately we tend to reuse the same passwords and codes – which lessens the security. With practice, however, it's not too hard to learn new passwords and PINs, improving the security of our various accounts.

Spend a few moments focusing on these examples below, then cover them over and see how accurately you can recall them.

Email: b34n13m34n13

Door code: 1147A

Credit-card PIN: 0142

Telephone-banking PIN: 8211

Voicemail: sausage135

Are you ready? Cover over the top half of the page, then try to recall as many of the passwords as you can:

Credit-card PIN: _____

Voicemail: _____

Door code: _____

Email: _____

Telephone-banking PIN: _____

How did you do? If you couldn't remember any of them, take a break for now but return and try this exercise another time.

Fruit Salad

Can you remember all of the ingredients the chef needs for his fruit salad? Have a look at the list below, and try to remember the number of each kind of fruit required. After about 60 seconds, cover the list and try to recall the quantities in the spaces provided below.

4 apples

4 bananas

11 pears

60 grapes

2 mangoes

7 pineapples

6 melons

3 oranges

Now cover over the list and write how many of each fruit are needed:

_____ grapes	_____ mangoes
_____ pears	_____ melons
_____ apples	_____ pineapples
_____ oranges	_____ bananas

Kings and Queens

Can you use some of the techniques you have learned so far to create a method for remembering the list of British kings and queens, in the order they reigned, below? There's no need to learn the years too. You could try an acrostic, perhaps, or maybe a rhyming poem. (If you already know the list of monarchs, try memorizing the years that each monarch came to the throne instead).

Anne (1707)

George I (1714)

George II (1727)

George III (1760)

George IV (1820)

William IV (1830)

Victoria (1837)

Edward VII (1901)

George V (1910)

Edward VIII (1936)

George VI (1936)

Elizabeth II (1952)

Use the space below to make a note of your memorization method for the list in order. When you are ready, cover this page and read the next page.

_____

_____

_____

Kings and Queens (continued)

Make sure you have completed the opposite page, and then cover it over.

Now that you have learned the list of kings and queens of Britain, can you recall them in order? Two are given below to help you out, but can you complete the rest of the list?

_____

_____

_____ George II (1727) _____

_____

_____

_____

_____ Victoria (1837) _____

_____

_____

_____

_____

_____ Elizabeth II (1952) _____

By George! How did you do?

Hints and Tips

Emotional Connections

» The events which are most memorable to us are those that are associated with strong emotions – whether good or bad. This is why you probably remember where you were and what you were doing when major world events took place, such as the Moon landings (if you are old enough). This is also why personal memories are often strongly retained, and why you are likely to always recall at least some aspects of your wedding day, or perhaps some details of a terrible argument you once had.

» Knowing that emotional events are memorable, you can take advantage of this by making something more meaningful or interesting to help commit it to memory. This doesn't mean creating heavily emotional memories, which would be extremely tiring, but rather finding quirky or amusing connections. Luckily, that type of emotion is also memorable! Of course, these connections will sometimes be unique to your personality, so what works for you will not necessarily work for other people.

» One way to remember something is to try find a way of making it funny to you. For example, if you're trying to remember that the symbol for Gold is Au, you could remember the funny sentence, "Au, gimme that gold!"

» Alternatively, it helps to make something easier to later recall if you deliberately associate it with something that you find easier to remember. For example, try connecting a series of facts with a funny story, so the facts "take place" in the story as it goes. This warmer, more "emotional" presentation gives the story a natural memorability.

Word Order

Look at the following list of toys for up to 60 seconds, and try to remember
exactly where they appear in this table. Then, when the time is up, cover them
over and see if you can place them back into their original positions in the empty
table at the bottom of the page. You will be given the list of toys to help remind
you.

Ball	Doll	Model
Kite	Puzzle	Soldier
Train set	Rocking horse	Teddy

Now, cover over the above and try to put the toys back in their right places.

The toys to place are:

Kite	Doll
Teddy	Rocking Horse
Model	Train set
Ball	Puzzle
Soldier	

_____	_____	_____
_____	_____	_____
_____	_____	_____

Added Flowers

Cover over the opposite page, then take some time to study the flowers below.

The differences between the plants are obvious, but perhaps somewhat hard to memorize, so it might help to describe each flower to yourself in some detail.

Once you feel you have memorized the flowers, continue on the opposite page.

Added Flowers (continued)

Cover over the opposite page and reveal this one.

The pictures below include *all* of the images that you saw on the opposite page, but there are now four extra, new images. Can you circle all of them?

Address Book

Can you remember a few of these key contacts' details from the address book entries below? Cover the opposite page and then familiarize yourself with the information on this one. When you are ready, cover this page instead and try to fill in the missing details on the next page.

Freddy Green   42 Forrest Hill, London, UK
                      freddy@freddygreen.com

James Jameson   54a Colder Green, Birmingham, UK
                      jammyjamjam@gmail.com

Cherry Lynch   Apartment 1101, Fairfax St, LA
                      cherrytreelane@hotmail.com

Bud   Boulder House, Woodland Vale, OH
                      winnerkid101@ohioking.com

Steve Hudcsz   7990 N. Main St, New York, NY
                      stevenhudcsz@goldpartners.com

Maria Argez   maria@maargez.tv

Annie Smythe   Old Oak Farm, Cheshire, UK
                      farmerannie@cheshireoak.co.uk

Address Book (continued)

Now that you are familiar with the address book details on the previous page, try to fill in the missing contact details below.

Freddy Green   42 _____, London, UK
                      _____

_____   54a Colder Green, Birmingham, UK
                      _____

_____   _____, LA
                      cherrytreelane@hotmail.com

Bud   _____, Woodland Vale, OH
                      winnerkid101@_____

Steve _____   7990 N. Main St, New York, NY
                      _____

Maria Argez   _____

_____   _____
                      _____

How did you get on? You probably didn't remember every detail, but give it another try later on.

Easter Parade

Start by covering over the opposite page.

Below are nine pictures connected to the celebration of Easter. On the opposite page are the same pictures, but in a different order. Study the images below for up to 30 seconds, and try to memorize the order they are arranged in. Then cover them over and reveal the page opposite.

Easter Parade (continued)

Make sure you have completed and covered over the previous page first.

Now, can you draw lines to attach each image to the position it originally occupied on the previous page? For example, if you think the top-left image was previously arranged in the middle of the middle row, then draw a line from the top-left image to the middle box on the middle row.

Hints and Tips

Remembering Text

» Sometimes you might need to commit a passage of text to memory. Maybe you are giving a speech at a friend's wedding, and don't want to improvise as you go, or you are keen to learn a presentation for work. Alternatively, perhaps you are a performer and need to memorize a script.

» Some types of texts will need to be memorized word for word, while for others you need only remember the main points and perhaps your opening and closing sentences. Regardless of what you need to learn, there are techniques which you can use to help you.

» Make text easier to learn by separating it into sections, if it is not already. Once you have divided the text into sections, you should create a prompt or trigger for each section to help you remember the rest of the text. For example, if you have a speech or presentation to learn, you can write triggers on key cards. They can simply be written topic subjects, along with the most important points not to forget. Or, if you don't want any written notes, find a memorable way of connecting the end of one topic into the start of the next. Alternatively, you could memorize the list of topics itself.

» If there are certain key points you definitely need to not forget, make sure you focus in particular on these.

» If it is necessary to learn verbatim passages of text, start by repeating and rehearsing the first line of each section until it is completely committed to memory. Use repetition techniques to learn each line as well as you can - so, for example, be sure to revisit the text an hour, a few hours, and a day later to help reinforce the memories.

A Poem

Spend a few minutes looking at the poem below and trying to memorize it. When you feel you are ready, cover this page and try to recite the poem.

Once there was a slinky fox

With ginger-cinnamon fur,

Her eyes were green, with sparkly glints,

And her smile was just for her.

She'd creep along the fence at night,

And howl up to the moon,

The males would watch, all deep in love,

And each of them would swoon.

The vixen, no, she wouldn't look

At any of those cads,

She'd rather just sing to the moon

Than make those foxes dads.

Next, once you are confident that you know the poem, see if you can recite it to someone else!

A Tale of Two Cities

One of the most famous opening passages of any book is the start of *A Tale of Two Cities*, by Charles Dickens.

Read the following, and try memorize it word-by-word. Then, when you think you are ready, cover it over and try to write it out verbatim on the opposite page.

It was the best of times, it was the worst of times, it was the age of wisdom, it was the age of foolishness, it was the epoch of belief, it was the epoch of incredulity, it was the season of Light, it was the season of Darkness, it was the spring of hope, it was the winter of despair, we had everything before us, we had nothing before us, we were all going direct to Heaven, we were all going direct the other way – in short, the period was so far like the present period, that some of its noisiest authorities insisted on its being received, for good or for evil, in the superlative degree of comparison only.

A Tale of Two Cities (continued)

Complete the exercise on the opposite page first, then cover it over.

Now, can you write out the opening of *A Tale of Two Cities* below?

_____

_____

_____

_____

_____

_____

_____

_____

_____

_____

_____

_____

_____

_____

_____

_____

_____

_____

_____

Time for Tea

Have a look at the list of types of cake below. After a few moments, cover the list and look at the list on the bottom half of the page. You will be asked to identify which of the previously given types of cake are missing from the list.

Angel	Christmas
Upside-down	Chocolate
Carrot	Fairy
Gingerbread	Panettone
Battenberg	Apple
Birthday	Lemon
Marble	Eccles

Now that you are familiar with the list of cakes, cover them over and look at the list below. Can you say which cakes are missing?

Panettone	Eccles
Angel	Upside-down
Marble	Christmas
Apple	Chocolate
Gingerbread	Birthday

Memory Sums

This page contains two separate puzzles, divided by a line.

For each puzzle, start by covering over the second row of numbers. Then, study the top set of three numbers for just five seconds.

When five seconds are up, cover the first row and simultaneously uncover the second row. Using just your memory to recall the original numbers, which of the new numbers in the second row can be formed by *adding* together two of the numbers from the first row?

Once you have decided, check back to the original numbers. Were you right?

Next, repeat with the second puzzle on the page.

Row 1 – numbers:

7 10 12

Row 2 – totals to form:

16 19 21

Row 1 – numbers:

24 31 46 53

Row 2 – totals to form:

56 71 77 85

Turn to the final page of the book to check the solutions.

Hints and Tips

Visualization of Memories

» Sometimes you can't remember something, even when you are sure that you *do* know it. The "tip of the tongue" word phenomenon is a good example of this. So, it's all very well having a memory, but we also need to be able to *retrieve* it. In fact, some people think that we don't necessarily forget old memories but simply lose the ability to retrieve them. One key to being able to retrieve a memory is for it to have rich and meaningful associations with other memories, so that as you start to think about related memories it becomes easier to recall.

» You can sometimes make a memory richer and more connected by learning more about a subject, but this won't work for everything – so in these cases you could try visualizing what it is that you want to memorize. This doesn't require you to actually draw something, and you don't even need to perfectly imagine whatever it is you're trying to remember. You can simply use visual concepts to represent the memory, in whatever way makes sense. These will not only help you learn the memory in the first place, but may also make it easier to recall too.

» Visualization can work for connecting facts too. For example, if you want to remember that Vincent van Gogh was from the Netherlands, you could imagine an ear in a field of tulips. This way you are making a strong visual connection between Van Gogh (who lost his ear) and tulip fields (which are a hallmark of the Netherlands), and thus tying the two together.

» You can create crazy visualizations if you like. Just as funny and amusing descriptions can make something more memorable, so a funny or amusing visual image (or even a sequence of events) can be extremely memorable too.

» You can also use visualizations to remember lists, by finding amusing visual connections from one object to the next.

Accessorize and Visualize

Have a look at the 12 accessories listed below, and try to learn what they are.
It might help to visualize them as you do this, and perhaps to find a visual
connection from one to the next. For example, perhaps the necklace is looped
through the earrings?

When you feel sufficiently familiar with them, cover them over and look at the
bottom half of the page.

Necklace	Bow tie
Earrings	Headband
Ring	Anklet
Belt	Scarf
Cap	Gloves
Monocle	Cufflinks

Cover the top half of the page, and see if you can write it out again below:

_____   _____

_____   _____

_____   _____

_____   _____

_____   _____

_____   _____

Underground Stations

Cover over the opposite page, and then have a look at the London Underground stations below.

Spend as long as you need familiarizing yourself with this list. Then, when you are ready, cover over this page and look at the opposite page. You will be asked to identify which stations are now missing, and which ones have been added in their place.

Covent Garden

Bond Street

Warren Street

Holborn

Green Park

Charing Cross

Hyde Park Corner

London Bridge

King's Cross

Russell Square

Westminster

St Paul's

Piccadilly Circus

St James' Park

Underground Stations (continued)

Did you try to memorize all of the London underground stations on the previous page? If not, go back and look at that page first.

Now, cover over the previous page and see if you can spot which stations below were not in the original list – and which from the original list are now missing.

Bank

Euston

Covent Garden

Marble Arch

Holborn

Tottenham Court Road

King's Cross

Russell Square

London Bridge

Westminster

St Paul's

Charing Cross

Warren Street

Bond Street

Can you remember which stations are missing? Write them here:

_____

_____

Once Upon A Time

Cover over the bottom half of the page, then have a good look at the list of fairy-tale characters below. After 30 seconds, cover them over and reveal the bottom half of the page.

Cinderella	Big Bad Wolf
Hansel	Goldilocks
Rapunzel	Sleeping Beauty
Wicked Witch	Three Bears
Rumpelstiltskin	Jack

Now take a look at the list below. Can you say which of the fairy-tale characters have been replaced – and by whom?

Gretel	Rumpelstiltskin
Sleeping Beauty	Jack
Snow White	Goldilocks
Big Bad Wolf	Cinderella
Three Little Pigs	Rapunzel

Pictures and Words

Start by covering over the bottom half of the page, then notice how each of the six images below has a word next to it. Take some time to study the pictures and words, making an effort to remember which word is associated with which picture. Once you think you have learned the associations, cover them up instead and continue reading below.

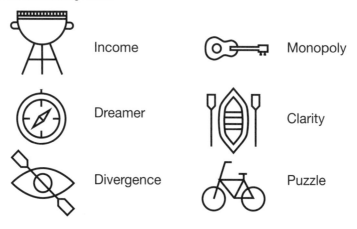

Income

Monopoly

Dreamer

Clarity

Divergence

Puzzle

Written below are the six words that were given at the top of the page. Can you now draw lines to join each word to the same image that it was originally next to?

Clarity   Divergence   Dreamer

Income   Monopoly   Puzzle

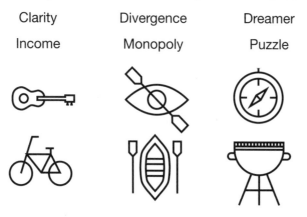

Lots of Lunches

Read the text below carefully and, when you feel you are sufficiently familiar with it, cover this page and see if you can answer the questions on the page opposite.

Dani the nanny looked around at the children as they hollered about lunch. So many different little faces wanting different things! She thought for a moment before raising both of her hands to quieten them all before calling out,

"Now who wants fajitas?"

Bobby, Sammy and Bill all raised their hands in joy, but Marie pulled a face.

"Yuck!" she exclaimed. "I want pasta!"

"I like pasta!" squealed TJ. "Pasta for me!"

More hands shot up, and the twins both pleaded simultaneously, "Pasta, pasta with cheese! Please!"

Dani nodded, making quick notes in her head. "Pasta for Marie, TJ, Caitlyn and Vik," she counted on her fingers. That was almost everybody covered, and she checked through each of them before spotting Lola seated in the corner.

"What about you Lola, what would you like?"

The little girl tugged at her hair for a moment thoughtfully, then clapped her hands together. "I want chocolate!"

Lots of Lunches (continued)

Have you read the story on the page opposite? If not, go back and read it before attempting to answer the questions on this page. Now you are familiar with the story, see if you can answer the following questions.

1. What meals are mentioned in the story?

_____

2. What are the names of the twins?

_____

3. Where is Lola sitting?

_____

4. What does Lola decide she would prefer to eat?

_____

5. Which children want to eat Mexican food?

_____

6. Who is looking after the children?

_____

7. How many children is the nanny looking after?

_____

Hints and Tips

Memorizing Numbers

» Occasionally it may be useful to remember certain numbers, such as a hotel room number, airport gate number, or an appointment time or number. Unfortunately we get into the habit of storing most numerical information in written form, which means we get little practice at doing this and can therefore struggle when we need to do so. Therefore, it's a good idea to try remembering numbers even when you don't need to, so you are better prepared whenever it becomes a necessity to do so. It's also wise to memorize some key phone numbers in case of emergency, in any case.

» Not all numbers need to be remembered for a long time, but if for example someone tells you a date they are coming to visit, or gives you a price quote over the phone, you may need to remember these for a short while until you have a chance to make a written note. Luckily, there are some simple techniques you can use to make it easier to remember numbers.

» One useful technique is to connect a string of digits to something you already know. For example, the number 1,945 is more easily remembered as the year 1945 – so for example as a reference to the end of the Second World War. It is even easier when we can connect a number to a personal date, such as a birthday of a loved one.

» Another way to deal with larger number sequences is to find a phrase with words whose length in letters correspond to the digits that make up the number. For instance, you could remember the number 353,927,194 by using the phrase 'How merry can Christmas be, without a Christmas tree?'

Number Memory

Try out the techniques discussed on the opposite page by seeing if you can memorize the following list of numbers. Use the space to the right of each number to make notes of how you can connect it to more memorable, associated concepts.

23 _____

18 _____

150 _____

2,001 _____

40 _____

2,512 _____

Now cover over the above and see if you can recall all six of the numbers:

_____

_____

_____

_____

_____

_____

Poetry Poser

Try learning this classic poem. You may need to repeat parts of it many times, perhaps breaking it down line by line, until you can recall it all without effort.

If you struggle, you might also try remembering just the first word of each line, since this may be sufficient to prompt you of the rest of the line once you start to become familiar with the poem.

Sonnet 18 – by William Shakespeare, 1564–1616

Shall I compare thee to a summer's day?

Thou art more lovely and more temperate.

Rough winds do shake the darling buds of May,

And summer's lease hath all too short a date.

Sometime too hot the eye of heaven shines,

And often is his gold complexion dimm'd;

And every fair from fair sometime declines,

By chance, or nature's changing course, untrimm'd;

But thy eternal summer shall not fade,

Nor lose possession of that fair thou ow'st;

Nor shall Death brag thou wander'st in his shade,

When in eternal lines to Time thou grow'st;

    So long as men can breathe, or eyes can see,

    So long lives this, and this gives life to thee.

Memory Sums

This page contains two separate puzzles, divided by a line.

For each puzzle, start by covering over the second row of numbers. Then, study the top set of three numbers for just five seconds.

When five seconds are up, cover the first row and simultaneously uncover the second row. Using just your memory to recall the original numbers, which of the new numbers in the second row can be formed by *adding* together two of the numbers from the first row?

Once you have decided, check back to the original numbers. Were you right?

Next, repeat with the second puzzle on the page.

Row 1 – numbers:

10 17 21

Row 2 – totals to form:

38 41 48

Row 1 – numbers:

5 8 13 16

Row 2 – totals to form:

15 19 21 28

Turn to the final page of the book to check the solutions.

Word Order

Cover over the bottom half of the page, then study the following table of currencies for up to 60 seconds. Try to remember exactly where they appear in this table. Then, when the time is up, cover them over and see if you can place them in the same positions in the empty table at the bottom of the page. You will be given the list of currencies to help remind you.

Lira	Kyat	Real
Pound	Rupee	Dollar
Zloty	Yen	Peso
Franc	Rand	Euro

Now, try to put the currencies back in their right places. They are:

Dollar	Euro	Franc
Kyat	Lira	Peso
Pound	Rand	Real
Rupee	Yen	Zloty

_____	_____	_____
_____	_____	_____
_____	_____	_____
_____	_____	_____

Directions

Can you memorize the following directions? To help learn them, you might make some written notes on the ruled lines below, or perhaps draw a brief diagram in the space given.

To get to the Annual Cake Party, turn left at French's coffee shop. Drive three miles, then take the second exit towards the beach. After about a mile, take the second right after Bear Rock and then the first left. You'll see the marquee for the Cake Party on the right.

Use this area to make written notes:

_____

_____

_____

_____

Or you could draw a diagram here:

Now cover over the page, and see if you can recall the route.

Hints and Tips

» It can be difficult to learn long sequences of digits or letters, but one way of simplifying this is to break these up into chunks that are easier to remember. This process of simplifying and compressing information is called "chunking".

» Our brain automatically chunks some information. For example, when we read or write a telephone number, we recite it in smaller groups to make it easier to follow. Similarly, we would usually read the year 1990 as "nineteen ninety" and not "one, nine, nine, zero".

» Chunking works well for long numbers, and can be particularly easy when the digits include familiar dates or years - so, for example, the number "231-9690-011" could perhaps be more easily memorized as "23", "1969", and "0011. If someone you know was born on the 23rd, that could cover the "23", and then the "1969" could be represented by the first man on the moon. Finally, the "0011" could be memorized by noting that it's a sequence of two repeated digits, starting as low as you can go.

» Chunking information not only makes it easier for you to learn but it also makes it easier to recall the knowledge at a later stage, since you have a stronger connection to it than you would otherwise have.

» Some groups of information are harder to associate with other concepts, so some people facilitate their memory of long numbers by pre-learning connections. For example, perhaps you decide in advance that "3" is always a cat, "5" is a soldier, and "0" is a hole. Then, to remember, 530 you would think about a soldier picking up a cat, but accidentally falling down a hole in the process. This strong visual image makes the number massively more memorable – even to the point that you may well remember it some time later, with remarkably little effort. You just need to put in the effort once, in advance, to learn the image (or images) you choose to associate with each number.

Number-chunking Memory

Try out the techniques discussed on the opposite page by memorizing each of the following numbers.

Start by memorizing this first number and then, when you think you are ready, cover it over and see if you can rewrite it in the space given below:

346,987,123

_____

Now try remembering this much longer number, and then once you are ready cover it over and see if you can recall it:

130,019,922,005

_____

Finally, see if you can memorize – and then recall – these three numbers:

22,456

19,990,011

357,913,570

_____   _____

_____

Sports Test

Cover over the opposite page, then read and familiarize yourself with the list of sports below. Try to remember as many as you can.

On the next page, you will find a similar list of sports, with some extra ones inserted.

Archery	Fencing
Windsurfing	Karate
Judo	Dressage
Golf	Football
Lacrosse	Polo
Badminton	Cricket
Rugby	Basketball
Orienteering	Skiing
Baseball	Biathlon
Swimming	Diving

Once you are ready, cover over the list and reveal the following page.

Sports Test (continued)

You should read the opposite page first, if you have not done so already.

Now, have a look at the list below. Which of these sports has been added, relative to the list on the previous page? Circle the new additions.

Archery	Badminton
Baseball	Basketball
Biathlon	Cricket
Cycling	Discus
Diving	Dressage
Fencing	Football
Golf	Gymnastics
Judo	Karate
Lacrosse	Orienteering
Polo	Rugby
Skiing	Swimming
Tennis	Windsurfing

Image Array

Cover over the opposite page.

Now, look at the following 16 pictures. Spend as long as you feel you need memorizing them. Then, cover them over and turn to the next page where you will be asked to identify which images are missing.

Image Array (continued)

Start by reading the opposite page. If you have already done so, then make sure the opposite page is covered and continue reading.

There were 16 pictures on the previous page, but there are only 12 on this one. Can you recall and then write down descriptions of the four items that are now missing? Or, if you prefer, then feel free to make a drawing of them instead in the space provided.

Hints and Tips

Creating Connections

» You will have learned and then remembered a great many things throughout your life, but it can often be tricky to retrieve those memories. This is why it's important to connect memories together as much as possible. You can do this both explicitly, by looking for ways to connect them, and implicitly, by engaging with a subject and expanding your knowledge of it.

» As an example, say that you want to remember that the capital of Morocco is Rabat. That, as a standalone fact, has no particular meaning if you are not already familiar with either Morocco or Rabat. But, if you start to learn a bit about the country or the city, suddenly it isn't a disconnected fact but rather part of a body of knowledge about that country. Learn enough information about them, and soon the connection between Morocco and Rabat will be almost as unforgettable to you as other world capitals that you are extremely familiar with.

» Creating connections places something in context, so not only is it easier to retrieve – via those connections – but also makes it more meaningful and therefore interesting. Your brain likes interesting things, and is more likely to remember them than seemingly unimportant, abstract facts.

» It isn't always possible to learn a lot about subjects, but it's always good to try and place some new information in context if you can. The more you can connect information into an overall set of knowledge, the easier it is to learn, to retain, and to retrieve.

Raising the Bar

Can you remember the following drinks order? Have a look at the order below.

2 vodka and cola

1 brandy with ice

3 rum and orange juice

1 soda and lime cordial

4 sambuca

2 manhattans

Now cover the order and see if you can rewrite the six drinks, along with their quantities, on the lines provided.

_____

_____

_____

_____

_____

_____

Did you remember all of the drinks, and the correct number of each?

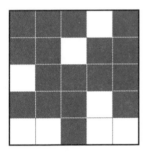

Grid Memory

Look at the pattern in the first grid on the left of the page, then cover it over and see if you can accurately reproduce it in the empty grid on the right of the page. Then, once you're done, repeat with the other grid.

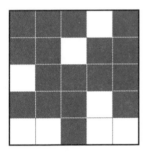
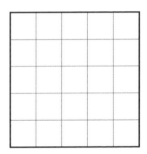

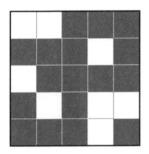
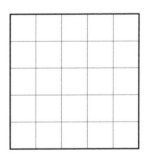

How Puzzling!

Have a look at the list of puzzle types listed below. After a minute, cover the list and study the bottom half of the page. Which puzzle types have been inserted into the list?

Bridges	Clouds
Hanjie	Yajilin
Futoshiki	Sudoku
Wordsearch	Four winds
Maze	Tapa
Anagram	Masyu

When you are ready, cover over the list above. Now, read the list below and circle the puzzle types that did not appear above.

Anagram	Bridges
Clouds	Four winds
Futoshiki	Hanjie
Hitori	Kakuro
Lighthouses	Masyu
Maze	Sudoku
Tapa	Walls
Wordsearch	Yajilin

Guest List

Take a good look at the list of names below. After a couple of minutes, cover over the list and take a look at the opposite page.

Harry	Sam
James	Olivia
Leo	Chloe
Tommy	Sophie
Kim	Lily
Katie	Bob
Bill	Amelia
Charles	Megan
Damon	Annie
Steve	Isabella
Ted	Philip
Neil	Holly
Kate	Summer
Eloise	Poppy

Guest List (continued)

Now, cover over the names on the opposite page and look at the list below.

The list is in the same order, but some of the names have been replaced with other names. Can you circle the names that have changed?

Harry	Ava
James	Florence
Leo	Chloe
Noah	Sophie
Kim	Lily
Katie	Bob
Bill	Oscar
Charles	Megan
Damon	Annie
Freddie	Isabella
Ted	Philip
Neil	Evelyn
Kate	Summer
Eloise	Poppy

Hints and Tips

» A powerful technique for learning lists of items is to use what are called "memory pegs". In this technique, you pre-learn a set of "pegs" which have the potential to connect to a wide range of other items. Then, when you want to remember a list, you simply "hang" each item on a "peg". Later, when you want to retrieve the list, you revisit your pre-learned pegs and take a look at what's hanging on each peg.

» This technique solves one of the key problems of remembering: finding a way to retrieve something. By spending the effort upfront to strongly learn the actual pegs, you can then harvest that effort for evermore by relying on the fact that you won't forget them.

» A peg can be anything you like, but ideally it will provide a lot of potential ways to connect to any of the sorts of thing you would like to remember. It will help if you can clearly visualize it, and if you can find an amusing way to connect it to items. So, for example, you might have a peg that is a walking stick. If you want one day to remember "orange", you could imagine a walking stick being used to play hockey with an orange as a ball, or a walking stick with an orange impaled on the bottom, and so on. Then, when later on you want to retrieve the memory, you think of "walking stick" (using your pre-learned peg) and hopefully that visual memory will have been interesting enough that you then immediately think "orange".

» The more pegs you create, the more things you can remember, and if you learn your pegs in a particular order then you can also use them to remember the order of a sequence.

» If you want to remember numbers using pegs, you'll have to devise a visual system for the numbers first, as discussed on a previous Hints and Tips page – or place items that sound like or otherwise remind you of those items on the pegs.

Using Memory Pegs

Here are eight potential memory pegs. To use this system in your day-to-day life it would make sense to pick eight pegs of your own choice, but, for the purposes of this puzzle, can you find a witty, amusing or clever way to attach each of the given items to its peg?

Peg	Item	Your connection
Walking stick	Doughnut	_____
Shoe	Toothbrush	_____
Wheelbarrow	Bread	_____
A door	Sausages	_____
Sticky notes	Cash	_____
Headphones	Rabbit	_____
Bus	Batteries	_____
Fountain	Apples	_____

Once you have written the connections, without any further memorization effort, try covering them over and see if you can use just the pegs to retrieve the items:

Walking stick	_____
Shoe	_____
Wheelbarrow	_____
A door	_____
Sticky notes	_____
Headphones	_____
Bus	_____
Fountain	_____

Vegetable Mix

Can you remember all of the ingredients the chef needs for his vegetable dish? Have a look at the list below, and try to remember the number of each kind of vegetable required. After about 60 seconds, cover the list and try to recall the quantities in the spaces provided below.

15 potatoes

3 cabbages

7 squashes

9 parsnips

5 yams

8 sweet potatoes

10 heads of broccoli

6 leeks

Now cover over the list and write how many of each vegetable are needed:

____ cabbages   ____ heads of broccoli

____ leeks   ____ parsnips

____ potatoes   ____ squashes

____ sweet potatoes   ____ yams

PINs and Passwords

We often need to recall passwords and PIN codes on a regular basis. Can you learn the following logins and codes? Spend as long as you need focusing on these, and then cover them over and see if you can recall them all.

Bank account PIN: 7761

Credit-card PIN: 1022

Social media login: rabbit8482

Shopping password: iastuy56

Security PIN: 1151

Are you ready? Cover over the top half of the page, then try to recall as many of the PINs and passwords as you can:

Bank account PIN: _____

Credit-card PIN: _____

Shopping password: _____

Security PIN : _____

Social media login: _____

How did you do? If you missed any of these, take another look later and try this exercise again.

Alice in Wonderland

Below are the opening lines from the novel *Alice's Adventures in Wonderland*, written by Lewis Carroll.

Test your memory skills by reading it through carefully, taking each word into consideration – but without rereading it. Then, when you have finished the passage, cover it over and read the instructions at the top of the opposite page.

Alice was beginning to get very tired of sitting by her sister on the bank, and of having nothing to do: once or twice she had peeped into the book her sister was reading, but it had no pictures or conversations in it, "and what is the use of a book," thought Alice "without pictures or conversations?"

So she was considering in her own mind (as well as she could, for the hot day made her feel very sleepy and stupid), whether the pleasure of making a daisy-chain would be worth the trouble of getting up and picking the daisies, when suddenly a White Rabbit with pink eyes ran close by her.

Alice in Wonderland (continued)

Start on the opposite page, if you have not yet completed the exercise there.

Making sure that you have covered over the text on the opposite page, read through the copy of it below. Eight words have been changed. Can you underline or circle them all? As a hint, four are in the first paragraph, and four can be found in the second paragraph.

Alice was starting to get very tired of waiting by her sister on the bank, and of having nothing to do: once or twice she had looked into the book her sister was reading, but it had no pictures or conversations in it, "and what is the use of a book," mused Alice "without pictures or conversations?"

So she was considering in her own mind (as well as she could, for the warm day made her feel very sleepy and slow), whether the pleasure of making a daisy-chain would be worth the effort of getting up and picking the daisies, when suddenly a White Rabbit with pink eyes hopped close by her.

Hints and Tips

Memory Palaces

» We have just looked at the "memory peg" technique, where items you wish to remember are assigned to a pre-learned set of objects. You can also do something similar with rooms, instead of objects, where you pre-learn a sequence of rooms and then you "place" the items you want to remember inside those rooms. You do this by finding a memorable visual connection, so for example you might place "ham" in your palace by imagining that the walls of one of the rooms are covered in ham instead of wallpaper.

» Using rooms, instead of pegs, has a big advantage – there is a natural connection between them, if you use rooms that you are already familiar with, which provides an easy-to-remember ordering – and is great for learning ordered lists. And, what's more, rooms are more complex than individual objects, so there is a greater range of options for connecting the items you wish to remember into the rooms.

» To create your memory palace, think about a building familiar to you. It could be your house or office building, or even your old school. Imagine walking through the building, considering the layout of the rooms and the route you would take to reach each one of them. Decide on a fixed route, and you're done: this is your memory palace.

» The number of items you can remember will be limited by the number of rooms in your palace, but you can always add on extra rooms – once you have allowed time to learn them. You could have your house connect into your office, or why not add a swimming pool or bowling alley into your memory palace? So long as you can clearly visualize it, it will work.

Using a Memory Palace

Start by reading the text opposite if you haven't already done so. Now, let's create an example memory palace, and try placing items into it. We'll write out the palace's rooms for now, but to use it yourself you'd need to create your own palace.

First, imagine yourself walking through your palace and placing the items you want to remember in the different rooms. The more unusual and amusing the placement, the more memorable it will be. For example, you may walk into the lounge and see giant cabbages used as coffee tables, if you want to remember "cabbage", or in the bedroom there could be sliced-cheese bed covers, if you want to remember "cheese".

Come up with your own connections for the following items:

Room	Item	Your connection
Hall	Necklace	_____
Lounge	Basketball	_____
Kitchen	Calendar	_____
Dining room	Crayons	_____
Stairs	Pizza	_____
Bedroom	Batteries	_____

Once you have written the connections, without any further effort, try covering them over and see if you can walk through your palace and retrieve the items:

Hall	_____
Lounge	_____
Kitchen	_____
Dining room	_____
Stairs	_____
Bedroom	_____

Banking Bonanza

Start by covering over the opposite page.

Below are 12 pictures related to banking and online banking. On the opposite page are the same pictures, but in a different order. Study the images below for up to 60 seconds, and try to memorize the order they are arranged in. Then cover them over and reveal the page opposite.

Banking Bonanza (continued)

Make sure you have completed and covered over the previous page first.

Now, can you draw lines to attach each image to the position it originally occupied on the previous page? For example, if you think the top-left image was previously arranged to the rightmost place on the middle row, then draw a line from the top-left image to the rightmost box on the middle row.

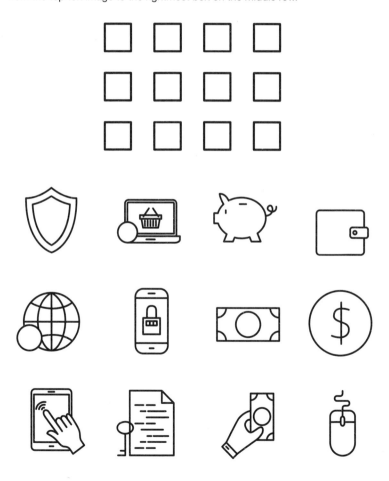

Facts about Egypt

Read the following list of facts about Egypt. Later, and perhaps again tomorrow or another day, come back and try the questions on the opposite page to see how much you recall.

- The largest Arabic population in the world is in Egypt.

- Pharaoh Pepi II reigned for 94 years, having become king at just six years of age.

- Only an inch of rain falls in Egypt every year.

- Egypt is formally known as the "Arab Republic of Egypt."

- The Great Pyramid at Giza took more than 20 years to build, and was built for the burial of King Khufu.

- Ramses II ruled Egypt for 60 years. He had over 90 children.

- There are more than 700 different Egyptian hieroglyphs.

- There are three Ancient Egyptian obelisks that are all referred to as Cleopatra's Needle. They are now in London, Paris and New York City.

Facts about Egypt (continued)

How is your memory for facts about Egypt? Find out by seeing how many of the following questions you are able to answer:

1. How many children did Ramses II have?

    _____

2. How old was Pharaoh Pepi II when he began his reign?

    _____

3. Where are the three Cleopatra's Needles now situated?

    _____

4. What is the formal name of the country of Egypt?

    _____

5. How much rain falls in Egypt every year?

    _____

6. Who was the Great Pyramid at Giza built for?

    _____

7. At least how many different Egyptian hieroglyphs are there?

    _____

Now go back and reread the facts again. How did you do?

Added Activities

Cover over the opposite page, then take some time to study the activities below.

The differences between the activities are obvious, but perhaps somewhat hard to memorize, so it might help to describe each activity to yourself in some detail.

Once you feel you have memorized the activities, continue on the opposite page.

Added Activities (continued)

Cover over the opposite page and reveal this one.

The pictures below include *all* of the images that you saw on the opposite page, but there are now four extra, new images. Can you circle all of them?

Hints and Tips

Memory Palaces with Pegs

» One of the most powerful memory techniques is created by combining the memory palace and memory peg systems. It works like the memory palace system, but, instead of only placing one item per palace room, you place a number of pegs into each room – and then you place items you wish to remember onto the pegs that are located in the rooms.

» Now, instead of imagining a route from room to room, you imagine a route through your palace that takes you from peg to peg. Therefore it makes sense for you to pick pegs that correspond with the real rooms on which your palace is based – or to place your imaginary pegs into actual, precise locations in the rooms. In this way you can still imagine yourself walking through the building, and you shouldn't fail to remember the order that you encounter each of the pegs in.

» As an example, if your memory palace initially consisted of passing from a hall into a lounge, your new memory palace with pegs would add some pegs into both the hall and lounge. You can add as many as you wish, and they can be whatever you like, although the same guidelines apply as for the original memory peg system. You will need to learn the palace-with-pegs only once, at least until you decide to add to it later, but the initial effort will be rewarded many times over as you start to use it. It's also possible to come back later and add further pegs into existing rooms, rather than having to add rooms onto the end of the palace. You can also redecorate, and change out pegs that are hard to use.

» Like all memory techniques, it will be slow-going at first, since it is only with familiarity that it starts to reward you – but once you finally have your route past all the pegs always ready to hand, and you have rehearsed adding things to the pegs in ways that work for you, then you will be able to remember long lists of items – accurately, in order, and with ease!

Item Tour

Try using the memory-palace-with-pegs technique to remember the following list of items.

You will first of all need to work out your memory palace. Some space is given first for you to write in an initial draft of a palace, but you will probably want to refine it over time if you start to use it for real-life memorization. Remember that you will probably want to place multiple pegs in each room, and for the journey through the palace to make logical sense.

Room	Peg

Now try using your palace-with-pegs to remember the following eight items:

Cat	Pencil
Crown	Laptop
Popcorn	Tennis ball
Lamp	Teddy bear

Having placed the items onto the pegs, cover over the list of eight items above and see if you can recall them just by revisiting the pegs listed at the top of the page.

Feeling Funny

Often it is easier to remember something when it invokes some sort of emotion, such as amusement.

Read the following jokes and puns, and spend a few minutes memorizing them. Then, when you think you are sufficiently familiar with them, close the book and see how many you can recite out loud.

- I used to be a banker – but then I lost interest.

- What happened when the red ship and blue ship collided at sea?
  All the sailors were marooned.

- Why did the cow win the Nobel Prize?
  Because it was out-standing in its field.

- What's brown and sticky?
  A stick.

- I didn't like my beard at first – but then it grew on me.

- Two parrots were on a perch. One said to the other: 'Can you smell fish?'

- Why did the door win the Nobel Prize?
  Because it only had a knocker.

High Spirits

Can you memorize the list of alcoholic spirits below? Look at them for a few moments, before covering them over and continuing reading on the bottom half of the page.

Absinthe

Amaretto

Bourbon

Cognac

Gin

Midori

Rum

Tequila

Vodka

Now, cover over the list above. Can you identify which spirits are missing from the following list?

Rum

Amaretto

Gin

Cognac

Vodka

Bourbon

Roman Emperors

Can you use some of the techniques you have learned so far to remember the list of Roman emperors below? You might consider an acrostic, perhaps, or a rhyme. (Note that there's no need to remember the years they were in power – these are included purely for interest's sake).

Caligula (37–41 AD)

Claudius (41–54 AD)

Nero (54–68 AD)

Galba (68–69 AD)

Otho (69 AD)

Vitellius (69 AD)

Vespasian (69–79 AD)

Titus (79–81 AD)

Domitian (81–96 AD)

Nerva (96–98 AD)

Trajan (98–117 AD)

Hadrian (117–138 AD)

Antoninus Pius (138–161 AD)

Lucius Verus (161–169 AD)

Marcus Aurelius (161–180 AD)

Use some spare paper to make a few notes to help you memorize the list in order. When you are ready, cover this page and head to the next page to test your recall skills!

Roman Emperors (continued)

Read the opposite page first.

Now you have learned some of the Roman emperors, can you recall them in order? We've given a couple to help you out, but can you complete the list?

Caligula (37–41 AD)
_____

_____

_____

_____

_____

_____

Titus (79–81 AD)

_____

_____

_____

_____

_____

_____

_____

Should you wish to make this even trickier, you can try to remember the years each emperor was in power too.

Flower Power

Take a good look at the list of flowers below. After a couple of minutes, cover over the list and take a look at the opposite page.

Carnation	Jasmine
Azalea	Daffodil
Magnolia	Lavender
Zinnia	Cyclamen
Gerbera	Lily
Pansy	Tulip
Snapdragon	Calla lily
Rose	Narcissus
Hibiscus	Hyacinth
Primrose	Delphinium
Violet	Stock
Daisy	Geranium
Lilac	Orchid
Freesia	Poppy

Flower Power (continued)

Now, cover over the flowers on the opposite page and look at the list below.

The list is in the same order, but some of the flowers have been replaced with other flowers. Can you circle the flowers that have changed?

Carnation	Jasmine
Azalea	Daffodil
Begonia	Lavender
Zinnia	Cyclamen
Alyssum	Lily
Wallflower	Tulip
Snapdragon	Calla lily
Mallow	Agapanthus
Hibiscus	Hyacinth
Primrose	Delphinium
Violet	Stock
Daisy	Geranium
Lilac	Orchid
Aster	Poppy

Hints and Tips

Your Train of Thought

» Do you ever find yourself struggling to remember what you were about to say? It's particularly annoying when you feel it was important, or embarrassing if it happens in the middle of a conversation – or presentation. Other times, you might walk into a room and discover you have forgotten why you went in there.

» Sometimes you lose your train of thought because you are doing things on autopilot, and aren't sufficiently focused. When you go into a room and have forgotten why, it's because you didn't make sure you were paying attention when you set off to the room. Next time, say out loud to yourself what you are going to do before you do it, and you will be far less likely to have forgotten already just a few moments later.

» In a conversation, we become distracted because we are trying to listen to what someone else says – or perhaps think of what we want to say in return, which in turn can flush our existing thought out of our head. One way to avoid this is to try and make the "good idea" we want to mention immediately more memorable, perhaps by rephrasing it in our minds or simply repeating it to ourselves.

» In a presentation situation, it may well be that the stress of the event is significant enough that it distracts us from what might otherwise have been a relatively simple task. The only way around this, unfortunately, is to prepare better – either by memorizing more effectively, or by writing a list of notes that can prompt you.

» If you do forget what you meant to say or do, then try not to worry what other people may think. Often they won't even notice – everyone else, after all, is caught up in their own mental struggle to pay attention, focus and remember the things they want to remember too!

Quick Recall

Read through this list of words slowly, trying to link them from one to another with memorable connections.

You can do this as slowly as you like, but once you've moved on to a word don't go back to a previous one. Then, when you reach the last word, cover them over and see if you can write out the entire list. You will be given the very first word, as a prompt.

Mouse	Hat	Smile
Dog	Umbrella	Food
Glass	Speech	Drop
Arrive	Monkey	Rain

Mouse	_____	_____
_____	_____	_____
_____	_____	_____
_____	_____	_____

Connections Challenge

You can use ridiculous or humorous connections to help make a list of items much more memorable. Consider the ten items in the list in the left column below, for example. Taken on their own, they might be hard to memorize, but if you try linking them in amusing ways it can get easier – then you just need to remember the first item, since the connections will be recalled more easily.

For example, starting from **computer**, it could be being operated by an **elephant** who is struggling to type with his giant paws, and is wearing a ridiculous **t-shirt**, and so on. The sillier the connections, the easier it will be to remember the list.

Write your own ideas for connections to the next item in the space to the right of each item:

Computer   _____

Elephant   _____

T-shirt   _____

Doughnut   _____

Boat   _____

Tower   _____

Diamond   _____

Custard   _____

Piano   _____

Washing machine   _____

When you have finished creating associations for each word, read over them to remind yourself of them, then cover the items. Now, how many of the items can you recall by starting from the first item: **Computer**

Memory Sums

This page contains two separate puzzles, divided by a line.

For each puzzle, start by covering over the second row of numbers. Then, study the top set of three numbers for just five seconds.

When five seconds are up, cover the first row and simultaneously uncover the second row. Using just your memory to recall the original numbers, which of the new numbers in the second row can be formed by *adding* together two of the numbers from the first row?

Once you have decided, check back to the original numbers. Were you right?

Next, repeat with the second puzzle on the page.

Row 1 – numbers:

13   15   18

Row 2 – totals to form:

25   28   38

Row 1 – numbers:

5   14   17   21

Row 2 – totals to form:

17   21   31   35

Turn to the final page of the book to check the solutions.

Tiger Watch

Carefully read the story below. Once you are familiar with the text, cover this page over and try to answer the questions on the opposite page.

He motioned for her to be silent by holding his finger to his lips and hushing her with the slightest of noises, before gesturing with his eyes towards the tiger. Aya peered forward through the undergrowth, trying to spot some birds, but it was impossible. She huffed impatiently.

"It's too overgrown!" she whispered sharply. Ray didn't dare take his gaze from the wild animal, but he motioned for her to be quiet. Aya, however, wasn't listening and wasn't looking. She was too busy trying to pick up her skirt and rearrange her bare feet enough to inch forward.

"Be quiet," he hissed, trying his hardest to make as little noise as he possibly could. He found himself gulping as the tiger raised its golden irises from the water where it had been drinking, and looked straight towards their spot, hidden among the jungle foliage. For one brief second, their gazes met and Ray instinctively grabbed for Aya's hand.

"Run!"

Tiger Watch (continued)

Did you read the story on the opposite page? If not, please go back and read the text before attempting this page.

Now that you have read the story, see if you can answer the questions below:

1. According to the story, what clothing is Aya wearing?

    _____

2. How are the tiger's eyes described?

    _____

3. Which two verbal commands does Ray give to Aya?

    _____

4. Which two movements does Ray use to try to keep Aya quiet?

    _____

5. What has the tiger been doing, before spotting Ray?

    _____

6. What was Aya trying to spot through the undergrowth?

    _____

Dinosaur Decisions

Spend a couple of minutes examining the list of dinosaurs below, then cover it
over, wait a few seconds, and then see how many you can write out again at the
bottom of the page. You'll be given the first letter of each dinosaur as a clue.

Triceratops	Stegosaurus
Velociraptor	Giganotosaurus
Diplodocus	Baryonyx
Pterodactyl	Spinosaurus
Dilophosaurus	Allosaurus

Now see how many dinosaurs you can recall:

T_____   S_____

V_____   G_____

D_____   B_____

P_____   S_____

D_____   A_____

Grid Memory

Look at the pattern in the first grid on the left of the page, then cover it over and see if you can accurately reproduce it in the empty grid on the right of the page. Then, once you're done, repeat with the other grid.

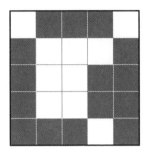
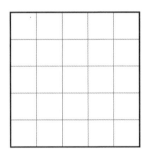

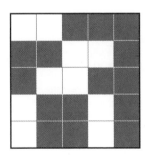
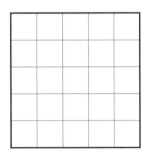

Hints and Tips

» Whether you are learning a new language, or you sometimes struggle to remember the spelling or meaning of words in your native language, there are memory techniques to help you.

» It is quite normal to get confused between homophone words such as principal and principle, or become unsure of how to spell tricky words. In these cases, if you know you have a particular weakness, don't be afraid to make use of various memory techniques to help you remember these slight differences and improve your language skills.

» You can create association links with homophone words to help you remember the differences. For example, you may want to associate the "a" in principal with the fact that it can be used as a noun: "**a** principal". This can also remind you that this is the correct spelling for the **a**djectival form of the word.

» If you are struggling to remember a word *at all*, then you can take advantage of the "tip of the tongue" effect in reverse, by running through the alphabet in your head and testing to see if the word starts with each letter in turn. As mentioned before, our memory seems to file words by their first letter, so this can act as a significant trigger to remembering the rest of the word. This technique can be particularly useful when solving word puzzles such as crosswords.

» Use rhymes or clever plays on words to make spellings and grammar more familiar and easier to learn. To remember the difference between "discrete" ("separate and distinct") and "discreet" ("respectful of privacy"), for example, you could note that the "e"s are kept separate in the second spelling – which fits nicely with its definition.

It's a Date!

You've received the following text message, but your device has just run out of battery and you can no longer read it.

Read through it a couple of times, then cover it over and see if you can still recall the correct information.

Hey there! It was great to meet you last night. I'd love to take you for lunch. How about 12.45 on the 19th August? There's a great place on the corner of 751 North St and 424 Main St. It's called *La Maison de Marie*. I'll book a table for the two of us. I'm in the office today so call me on 988-575-9976 to confirm. See you then! x

Are you ready? Cover the text above and see how many of the details you can still remember:

Suggested date: _____

Suggested time: _____

Restaurant name: _____

Restaurant location:

_____

Phone number: _____

Room for Dessert?

Have a look at this list of delicious desserts. Once you are familiar with it, cover this page over and look at the opposite page. Can you identify which desserts have been added?

Crepe	Apple pie	Cherry pie
Doughnut	Meringue	Profiterole
Fruit cake	Swiss roll	Waffle
Sponge	Peach turnover	Baked Alaska
Muffin	Cream puff	Chocolate cake
Cheesecake	Banoffee pie	Banana cake

Room for Dessert? (continued)

Read the opposite page first, then cover it over once you are done.

Have a look at the list below. Which desserts have been inserted into the list?

Apple pie	Baked Alaska	Banana cake
Banoffee pie	Cheesecake	Cherry pie
Chocolate cake	Cream puff	Crepe
Doughnut	Fruit cake	Gateau
Madeleine	Meringue	Muffin
Peach turnover	Profiterole	Simnel Cake
Sponge	Swiss roll	Tarte Tatin
Tipsy Cake	Turnover	Waffle

Image Array

Cover over the opposite page.

Now, look at the following 16 pictures. Spend as long as you feel you need memorizing them. Then, cover them over and turn to the next page where you will be asked to identify which images are missing.

Image Array (continued)

Start by reading the opposite page. If you have already done so, then make sure the opposite page is covered and continue reading.

There were 16 pictures on the previous page, but there are only 12 on this one. Can you recall and then write down descriptions of the four items that are now missing? Or, if you prefer, then feel free to make a drawing of them instead in the space provided.

Hints and Tips

» Sleep is an incredibly important factor in forming long-term memories. In fact, much of the process of storing memories happens while we are sleeping. During this time your brain creates and strengthens the associations required to form lasting memories. A lack of sleep, or heavily disturbed sleep, will therefore lead to impaired long-term memory.

» In particular, memories are filed during deep, non-REM sleep, so it's really important to make sure you have enough sleep. Most adults need at least seven hours sleep, and very few people can get by on much less. Many of those who think they can have simply learned to live with the effects of sleep deprivation.

» Sleep has a whole host of other benefits, beyond directly solidifying memories. If you don't sleep enough you will find it hard to focus, which will also significantly impair your ability to form lasting memories.

» Sleep also lets you brain learn from what has happened during the day. For example, if you are learning a physical skill – such as playing a musical instrument, or juggling – then you need to sleep between practice sessions to allow time for your brain to lay down the appropriate procedural memories. So while it may be said that practice makes perfect, there is no point doing too much in one session. Your brain needs to have time to process what it has learned, so there are diminishing returns to longer rehearsal sessions – quite apart from grown tired and distracted.

Greek Tragedy Characters

Take a few minutes to focus on these different Greek tragedy characters, then cover them over and see how many you can recall when prompted with the first letter of each of their names. Some of these have quite complex spellings, so try to be as accurate as you can.

Ajax

Electra

Iphigenia

Jocasta

Laertes

Orestes

Oedipus

Andromache

Philoctetes

Helen

Now, cover over the list above and try to recall them below:

H_____   A_____

P_____   E_____

A_____   I_____

O_____   J_____

O_____   L_____

The Vegetable Competition

Read the story below carefully, and then try to answer the questions on the following page.

Margaret held up her two pumpkins with great glee. "They won first prize, darling!" she exclaimed loudly to her husband Gerald. "They beat Christopher's, hands down!"

Christopher looked glum as he held up his own pumpkins. "I don't know what happened this year," he huffed. "We had a case of the slugs, don't you know, but I'm not sure if that was it."

Poor Polly didn't know where to look. Trying to jolly Christopher along, she picked up a large bunch of carrots of all different shades and admired the purple, florid rosette adorning them. "Aren't these yours, Christopher? They've won a special prize!"

Christopher looked over in surprise and his face lit up as he looked at the rainbow carrots she proffered towards him. "Why yes, they are mine! Hoorah!" he cheered. "We'll leave the pumpkins for the rabbits, and we'll take these home for tea!"

"Good-o," Polly smiled. "Do you have any walnuts? Maybe we can make a carrot cake in the morning."

The Vegetable Competition (continued)

Did you read the story on the previous page? If not, go back and read it before attempting this page.

Now you've read the story, cover the opposite page and try to answer the questions below.

1. What does Polly check Christopher has so that she can make a carrot cake in the morning?

_____

2. Whose pumpkins won first prize?

_____

3. Who is married to Gerald?

_____

4. What type of vegetable, other than a pumpkin, did Christopher grow for the competition?

_____

5. How is the special prize rosette described?

_____

6. What did Christopher decide to do with his pumpkins?

_____

Pictures and Words

Start by covering over the bottom half of the page, then notice how each of the six images below has a word next to it. Take some time to study the pictures and words, making an effort to remember which word is associated with which picture. Once you think you have learned the associations, cover them up instead and continue reading below.

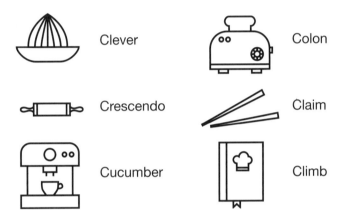

Clever

Colon

Crescendo

Claim

Cucumber

Climb

Written below are the six words that were given at the top of the page. Can you now draw lines to join each word to the same image that it was originally next to?

Claim   Clever   Climb

Colon   Crescendo   Cucumber

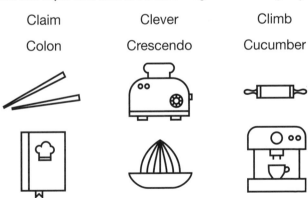

A Memory for Directions

Can you memorize these directions? If it helps, you could make some written notes on the ruled lines below, or maybe draw a brief diagram in the space given.

To get to the pet shop, walk through the village square and past the bakery. Turn left at the carpenter's and then take the next left when you see the flower market. Walk three blocks along, then pass beneath the bridge. Follow the path along until you see a statue of Shakespeare, and then you'll find the pet shop right behind him!

Use this area to make written notes:

_____

_____

_____

_____

Or you could draw a diagram here:

Now cover over the page, and see if you can recall the route on a blank piece of paper.

Hints and Tips

» With so much of our lives now digitally connected, we are constantly required to create – and recall – a wide range of usernames, passwords and PINs. Some of these will connect to accounts which contain very private or important information. And yet, despite this, our apparent lack of desire to take the time to learn more than one or two passwords leads to us taking huge security risks with our information – and all the aspects of our lives that connect to that information.

» If somebody breaches one of your accounts, would they be able to use that password to connect to others? If you have multiple accounts with the same login information – same username or same email address, with a matching password – then it's easier for someone to hack into your account. They only need to find the one weak link, which could happen through no fault of your own, and then they can use automated software to try a huge range of other sites to find anywhere else you have used the same information. Hacked accounts can also be used to impersonate people – which could have serious implications. And in some cases, such as with many popular devices, they can be used to remotely erase content, or access personal photographs, calendars, emails and so on.

» It's important, therefore, to remember a range of passwords, and ideally to never repeat the same username and password combination across any accounts, or at least to never do so with any account of even the slightest importance to you. Luckily, there are techniques which you can use to make a secure password without having to write it down. The most important step is to avoid dictionary words or common names, or versions of these where you have for example swapped numbers for letters. Even just a small deviation from a "standard" word can help. For example, you could add the first three letters or initials of the website to your generic password. So you might use "FBeggplant" for your Facebook account, instead of "eggplant". This helps to make it more secure while not complicating it so much that you'll forget it.

Passwords

One technique for remembering passwords is to use acrostics. So, for example, if you are trying to create a password for your online banking you could use something like "The money is hidden under my Sleepyhead mattress" to give you "TmihumSm" as a secure password. And the great advantage of an acrostic like this is that you can actually write it down somewhere, since no one would know what it means! You can add in digits or symbols, if required, too – symbols might be easier to add as words, such as "colon", however, rather than as actual symbols.

Use the acrostic technique, or some other method, to learn the following passwords. Note that using the acrostic technique working backwards from these is trickier than inventing your own acrostics and then extracting the passwords from them!

When you are done, cover them over and see how many you can recall.

Phone unlock: mmapd

Email account: luk-ttsof

Computer login: cupc4k*tw

Are you ready? Cover over the top half of the page, then see if you can recall these passwords:

Phone unlock: _____

Email account: _____

Computer login: _____

Dracula

Below are two paragraphs from the opening chapter of the novel *Dracula*, written by Bram Stoker.

Test your memory skills by reading it through carefully, taking each word into consideration – but without rereading it. Then, when you have finished the passage, cover it over and read the instructions at the top of the opposite page.

Count Dracula had directed me to go to the Golden Krone Hotel, which I found, to my great delight, to be thoroughly old-fashioned, for of course I wanted to see all I could of the ways of the country. I was evidently expected, for when I got near the door I faced a cheery-looking elderly woman in the usual peasant dress – white undergarment with long double apron, front, and back, of coloured stuff fitting almost too tight for modesty. When I came close she bowed and said, "The Herr Englishman?" "Yes," I said, "Jonathan Harker." She smiled, and gave some message to an elderly man in white shirt-sleeves, who had followed her to the door. He went, but immediately returned with a letter:

"My Friend. Welcome to the Carpathians. I am anxiously expecting you. Sleep well tonight. At three tomorrow the diligence will start for Bukovina; a place on it is kept for you. At the Borgo Pass my carriage will await you and will bring you to me. I trust that your journey from London has been a happy one, and that you will enjoy your stay in my beautiful land.

Your friend, DRACULA."

Dracula (continued)

Start on the opposite page, if you have not yet completed the exercise there.

Making sure that you have covered over the text on the opposite page, read through the copy of it below. Ten words have been changed. Can you underline or circle them all?

Count Dracula had directed me to go to the Silver Krone Hotel, which I found, to my great pleasure, to be thoroughly old-fashioned, for of course I wanted to see all I could of the ways of the country. I was evidently expected, for when I got near the hotel I faced a cheery-looking old woman in the usual peasant dress – dark undergarment with long double apron, front, and back, of coloured material fitting almost too tight for modesty. When I came close she curtsied and said, "The Herr Englishman?" "Yes," I said, "Jonathan Harker." She smiled, and gave some message to an elderly man in white shirt-sleeves, who had followed her to the door. He went, but immediately returned with a letter:

"My Friend. Welcome to the Carpathians. I am anxiously awaiting you. Sleep well tonight. At five tomorrow the diligence will start for Bukovina; a place on it is kept for you. At the Borgo Pass my carriage will await you and will bring you to me. I trust that your journey from London has been a happy one, and that you will enjoy your stay in my beautiful castle.

Your friend, DRACULA."

Animal Order

Look at the following list of animals on this page for up to 90 seconds, and try
to remember exactly where they appear in this table. Then, when the time is up,
cover them over and see if you can place them in the exact same positions in the
empty table on the opposite page. You will be given the list of animals to help
remind you.

Aardvark	Llama	X-Ray tetra
Kakapo	Buffalo	Manatee
Elephant	Jaguar	Donkey
Numbat	Zebu	Gopher
Reindeer	Crocodile	Hyena
Otter	Impala	Yak
Turkey	Vulture	Pheasant
Sheep	Quokka	Wolverine
Uakari	Ferret	

Animal Order (continued)

Now, try to put the animals back in their original places. The animals to place are:

Aardvark	Buffalo	Crocodile	Donkey	Elephant
Ferret	Gopher	Hyena	Impala	Jaguar
Kakapo	Llama	Manatee	Numbat	Otter
Pheasant	Quokka	Reindeer	Sheep	Turkey
Uakari	Vulture	Wolverine	X-Ray tetra	Yak
Zebu				

_____	_____	_____
_____	_____	_____
_____	_____	_____
_____	_____	_____
_____	_____	_____
_____	_____	_____
_____	_____	_____
_____	_____	

Memory Sums solutions

8.

1:
3 + 8 = 11

2:
13 + 22 = 35
17 + 22 = 39

68.

1:
7 + 12 = 19

2:
24 + 53 = 77
31 + 46 = 77

78.

1:
17 + 21 = 38

2:
5 + 16 = 21
8 + 13 = 21

112.

1:
13 + 15 = 28

2:
14 + 17 = 31
14 + 21 = 35